Challenging
PROJECTS
FOR CREATIVE MINDS

12 Self-Directed Enrichment Projects That Develop
and Showcase Student Ability

for Grades 1 to 5

by Phil Schlemmer, M.Ed., and Dori Schlemmer

Edited by Caryn Pernu

free spirit
PUBLiSHiNG®

Works
for kids™

At the time of this writing, all facts and figures cited are the most current available, and all Web site URLs are accurate and active. Please keep in mind that URLs change and sites come and go. When in doubt, use a search engine. NOTE: Parents, teachers, and other adults who are working with children using the Internet should make sure that the exploration of Web sites is age-appropriate and acceptable. We have done our best to identify sites that meet these criteria, but we cannot guarantee their contents.

Library of Congress Cataloging-in-Publication Data

Challenging projects for creative minds : 12 self-directed enrichment projects that develop and showcase student ability for grades 1 to 5 / by Phil Schlemmer and Dori Schlemmer ; edited by Caryn Pernu.

    p. cm.
   Includes bibliographical references and index
   ISBN 1-57542-048-1
   1. Education, Primary—Activity programs. 2. Education, Elementary—Activity programs. 3. Project method in teaching. 4. Creative activities and seat work. 5. Independent study. 6. Curriculum enrichment. I. Schlemmer, Phil. II. Schlemmer, Dori. III. Pernu, Caryn.
LB1537C54   1998   98-36249
372.13'6—dc21   CIP

10 9 8 7 6 5 4 3 2
Printed in the United States of America

Cover design by Circus
Book design and typesetting by Percolator
Illustrations by John C. Gerber
Index compiled by Diana Witt

Free Spirit Publishing, Inc.
400 First Avenue North, Suite 616
Minneapolis, MN 55401-1724
(612) 338-2068
help4kids@freespirit.com
www.freespirit.com

Acknowledgments

We want to thank the people who have helped in many ways to make this book a reality.

Elementary teachers in the Holland, Michigan, Public Schools have field-tested in various forms many of the ideas in the book. We appreciate their input, comments, and suggestions. A special note of appreciation goes to Anita Vanderhill, kindergarten teacher at Lincoln School in Holland, who helped conceptualize the Kids' Seed-Starter Kit.

Thanks to all of you for your help and support.

Contents

Introduction 1

Part 1: Living Things   7

Kids' Seed-Starter Kit (beginning level) 8
Students experiment with seeds and soil to develop a
Kids' Seed-Starter Kit.

This Place Is a Zoo! (intermediate level) 17
Student "wildlife experts" work for a local zoo designing
information for exhibits.

The Animal Inventor (advanced level) 27
Student "zoological advisers" create imaginary animals for
a science fiction movie.

Part 2: Numbers & Measurement   37

The School Sign Company (beginning level) 38
Students create signs that show distances within the
classroom and school.

School Census Bureau (intermediate level) 46
Students send Census Bureau Questionnaires to other
classrooms to collect data about the students in each grade.

Buying the Car of My Dreams (advanced level) 54
Students build a budget to buy the car of their dreams.

Part 3: People & Places   65

Home Sweet Home (beginning level) 66
Students create a classroom display depicting "Home Sweet Home."

American Heroes (intermediate level) 74
Students create stamps honoring their heroes.

Trading Card Hall of Fame (advanced level) 82
Students design trading cards of famous people and places
to be used as educational resources.

Part 4: Research 91

Did You Know? (beginning level) 92
Student teams produce educational collages to introduce their
classmates to a variety of topics and facts.

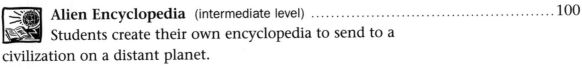
Alien Encyclopedia (intermediate level) 100
Students create their own encyclopedia to send to a
civilization on a distant planet.

Software Design Company (advanced level) 109
Student software developers design interactive educational
programs for a proposed new CD-ROM. (Note: Students do not need
to work on a computer to do this project.)

Part 5: Resources 127

Choosing a Topic 128
Finding Resources 129
Taking Notes 130
Planning Your Writing 131
A-OK Editing Checklist for Beginning Writers 132
A-OK Editing Checklist 133
Further Reading 134

Index 135
About the Authors 137

Introduction

The illiterate of the 21st century will not be those who cannot read and write,
but those who cannot learn, unlearn, and relearn.
—Alvin Toffler

Most people today recognize that students need to continue learning throughout their lives—a high school diploma, or even a college degree, is not the end of the education process. Students need opportunities to develop their personal strengths through studying topics that fit their needs and interests. They also need to learn strategies for finding relevant information, thinking critically, and transforming knowledge into something they can use for a specific purpose. Even—or perhaps especially—the youngest students need the experience of being in charge of their own school learning.

This book of performance-based projects offers educators a systematic way to provide both the *structure* and the *freedom* students need to become actively engaged in their own learning. Structure establishes clear guidelines and expectations. It outlines the concepts and principles the lesson is designed to teach. Freedom allows students to make some decisions about their own learning. They can explore their interests and develop their own unique strengths while learning the knowledge and skills their schools and communities deem important. Activities that stimulate students' imagination and creativity let them make personal contributions to their learning and discover their world in a new light.

Challenging Projects for Creative Minds is based on the concept of *authentic learning*. This means that students learn from assignments that provide a multifaceted, "real world" experience. The projects are based on concepts instead of facts. Rather than working on skill-and-drill assignments, students take control of the process. With your guidance, they gather information from a variety of sources, build on their existing knowledge, and connect this knowledge with the world outside the classroom. Authentic learning requires students to use a wide range of resources, activities, skills, and strategies. It opens the door for children to become passionate about a topic, explore its many facets, and share what they've discovered with pride and enthusiasm. The projects in this book tap into the idea of authentic learning.

Each of the twelve projects in this book contains the following components:

- A scenario that provides authentic reasons for doing the work and a context for student learning.

- Opportunities for students to study topics they find interesting, important, and relevant.

- Student handouts that provide the structure necessary for students to exercise freedom and independent thinking.

- A clearly defined final product that lets students demonstrate what they've learned.

- An assessment rubric that identifies critical skills, products, and knowledge students develop through the project.

- Standards of quality that outline the expectations for each component of the project.

- Extension possibilities for students who need additional challenges or more depth to their learning.

Because most elementary-school curricula stress structure over freedom, some people may question whether this type of learning is possible or even necessary for young children. Do first-graders have the capacity to make their own learning decisions? Shouldn't we wait until children have mastered basic skills and are mature enough to handle this kind of responsibility?

The fact is, children are self-directed learners from birth. They observe and listen and internalize what is going on around them to learn to talk. They diligently tackle difficult new skills like walking, and practice, practice, practice, until they've mastered the ability to go where they want to go. Parents give support and guidance as babies become toddlers, and toddlers soon become the children sitting in our classrooms. Elementary-school children need hands-on involvement with what they are learning. They enjoy projects they can initiate, plan, implement, and carry through. Education is about exploration and discovery. A child-centered curriculum helps you teach students that school can be a place where they have the opportunity to learn about what interests them and to develop their creativity. You can teach them how to find the information they need and why it's important. And they will understand that they can be self-directed, lifelong learners.

Whether you teach gifted and talented students, students with other special learning needs, or a "regular" class, you help students of different abilities and learning styles. No classroom is composed of students all at the same level of academic progress. Your students process information differently from each other and come to class with different experiences, background knowledge, and skills. All of these children need opportunities to develop their learning skills, but that's difficult to do in the classroom. *Challenging Projects for Creative Minds* can help you give students an active and responsible role in working with information. It provides structured projects that show students how to take charge of their own learning.

Goals

Because these projects are based on sound principles of learning, you'll find they can support the educational goals of students and schools—whether the projects are used with an entire classroom, as special small-group projects, or as extension activities for students who are motivated to learn more.

These projects allow STUDENTS to:

1. Direct their own learning through projects that allow them to make choices.

2. Develop practical and critical-thinking skills that they can apply to all areas of learning throughout their lives.

3. Develop self-confidence through completing a project that requires planning, problem solving, self-discipline, self-assessment, creativity, and presentation.

4. Develop ownership of their learning as they set and achieve personal goals.

5. Discover new abilities and interests, and practice skills.

6. Discuss their learning experiences and goals with others.

7. Develop a capacity for self-reflection and metacognition as they look back on their project and think about their work.

8. Present their projects to an audience.

9. Receive recognition for their work.

These projects allow TEACHERS to:

1. Offer project-based learning to all students or enrichment activities to students who need extra challenges.

2. Provide opportunities for students to develop their own strengths and direct their own learning.

3. Offer students choices and variety in their education.

4. Make better use of educational resources such as:

- spare class time (for students who complete assignments early)
- media center facilities
- technology (computers, software, Internet)
- student motivation
- untapped student potential
- basic skills and knowledge from the core curriculum

5. Showcase student abilities and achievements within both the classroom and the school.

6. Meet the needs of diverse learners.

7. Serve as an adviser or coach, working with individual students or small groups to check progress and encourage them to solve problems independently.

How to Use This Book

The materials in this book provide project-based learning opportunities for elementary students. The book is divided into four themes commonly found in the curriculum, and each theme includes a project at three different levels: beginning, intermediate, and advanced. You can select any project in the book, however, in any order, depending on your students' abilities and your classroom goals, since the materials are not linked or sequenced. You can easily modify the projects to serve students of different ages and abilities and adapt them to meet the specific content you need to teach.

Assignments

Each project begins with a brief introduction, an outline of the assignment, a list of the materials required, and a list of concepts students will study. Preteaching suggestions in the project steps help you prepare students to do the project. Some projects include important background information and suggested resources as well. Each activity is explained step by step and includes reproducible handouts to guide students in completing the assignment. You'll also find suggestions for adapting or expanding many activities beyond the classroom.

Assessment

A customized assessment form is included for each project. It organizes the assessment items into three areas:

1. Skills (I Used These Skills)
2. Products (I Made These Things)
3. Knowledge (I Learned These Things)

Because reflection and self-evaluation are important components of learning, students and their teachers are both asked to assess the finished projects. Students assess their own work based on the same criteria as the teacher uses , and they rate their work in each of these three areas.

The beginning level assessment form is less complex than the intermediate level or advanced level form. Younger children who aren't yet comfortable reading and writing may need to discuss the evaluation with an adult rather than write it down, while older children can complete an assessment on their own and discuss their perceptions with the teacher.

Be sure to include written comments pointing out what the student did well when you complete your assessment. Although writing out comments can be time-consuming and difficult, these are often the most important and memorable responses students get from teachers. Your qualitative responses give students a richer view of their accomplishments.

Standards of Quality

The "Standards of Quality," a detailed description of the expectations for each step of the project, can help you determine whether students have successfully completed the assignment. You can adapt the standards to reflect your own expectations for the project, should you decide to adjust the assignment in any way. Discuss these expectations with the students before they begin a project, so they clearly understand what they'll be doing and how their projects will be assessed.

Some teachers hold a class discussion to get students' ideas about what makes a project successful. This can be a great motivator, because students develop a greater sense of ownership and commitment to a project they've helped get started.

Classroom Extensions

Challenging Projects for Creative Minds is designed to help you extend your classroom curriculum. Extension projects provide students with learning opportunities that connect to the content they study but stretch beyond basic knowledge requirements. Their purpose is to "extend" the curriculum into areas that capture their interest and to motivate them to learn more. They add breadth, depth, and complexity to what students study.

There are many ways you can incorporate these kinds of extensions into your classroom program. Here are two of the most obvious:

1. Whole-class activity. As part of teaching a thematic unit, you may want to give students an opportunity to apply what they've learned. This type of extension, offered to all the students in the class, shows students how they can authentically use the information they've just learned.

For example, suppose you're teaching a social studies unit on your city or neighborhood and want to give students an opportunity to use their newly acquired knowledge. You could use the "Alien Encyclopedia" project (see pages 100–108) asking students to develop articles on an aspect of their community and display the finished book in the school's media center for everyone to read. Your students can share their new knowledge of their community in a product that demonstrates the value of what they've learned. In other words, the curriculum has been extended into a meaningful context for students. The engaging concept of alien communication provides a child-centered reason for applying real-world skills and knowledge to create a quality project.

2. Individual or group projects. At the outset of a new unit, you may determine (through a pretest or another method) that a number of students already understand the content or have mastered the outcomes the unit is designed to teach. You can offer these students an extension project that allows them to use what they already know in a more in-depth, complex way. This type of extension is meant to motivate and challenge students and give them work appropriate to their academic needs.

For example, suppose you're beginning a science unit on animals. Several students have already advanced beyond your planned curriculum in this area. They talk knowledgeably about animals and avidly read animal magazines and books such as *Ranger Rick* and the *Zoo Books* series. They already know everything you intend to teach the rest of the class and, in some cases, a lot more. You could use the project titled "This Place Is a Zoo" (see pages 17–26) to allow these students to work independently during class time.

If several students are working on the same extension, you can encourage them to work together or to discuss their project with each other to share ideas as they work. In this way, all students in the class study similar content, but the final outcomes better meet the needs of individual students. You can also make each extension student responsible for presenting what he or she learned to the class, increasing everybody's knowledge and understanding of the topic.

Getting Started

As a classroom teacher, you've accepted the challenge of helping prepare young children for life in this ever-changing world. You can help them gain experience completing performance-based projects that reflect the kind of skills they will need in the future—both inside and outside the classroom. The ready-to-use materials in this book provide the context and structure. Your students have the creativity and talent to meet the challenges. And you have an opportunity to help guide them in active learning experiences that will help them move from the concrete to the more abstract patterns of higher-order thinking skills. These projects have been designed to help you do that, to give your students exciting and creative opportunities to direct their own learning, build their confidence as learners, and, we hope, have some fun along the way.

PART 1

Living Things

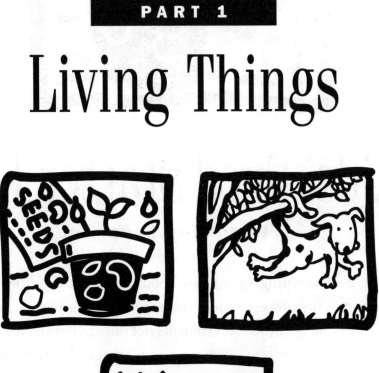

Kids' Seed-Starter Kit

Beginning Level

Starting seeds is a fascinating way to learn about plants and how they grow, especially when you watch the process closely and see something tender and green emerge from a tiny seed. This project introduces students not only to how plants grow from seeds but also to the process of scientific experimentation and close observation. Students will do research to develop a Kids' Seed-Starter Kit, using what they learn about plants and soil to assemble and design a kit that could be sold in stores.

This project involves the use of many materials. If you do it as a project for an entire classroom, you might want to set up one or two experiment stations rather than ask each student to conduct the experiment individually.

During the project students will:

1. Experiment with different seeds to decide which to include in a seed-starter kit.

2. Experiment with at least two types of soil to decide which to include in the kit.

3. Observe the seeds and plants at germination and various stages of growth.

4. Produce instructions for starting a seed.

5. Create a package to hold the Kids' Seed-Starter Kit, including seeds, paper towels, soil, and a container in which to plant the seeds.

MATERIALS

For each experiment station you set up you'll need:

- three paper towels
- three different kinds of seeds* (nine seeds of each kind)
- three sealable plastic bags
- masking tape for labels
- pencils or markers
- three cups of sand
- three cups of potting soil
- six small containers (such as paper cups)
- a measuring cup
- a teaspoon
- an eyedropper or pipette (you can use a plastic drinking straw cut in half)

For each completed Kids' Seed-Starter Kit you'll need:

- a bag or box to contain the final seed-starting kit
- crayons, paint, or art materials for decorating the kit's package
- a paper towel
- a cup of potting soil
- a paper cup to hold the soil
- an eyedropper or pipette (you can use a plastic drinking straw cut in half)
- six seeds (the type students chose as being best for the kit)
- a small container to hold the seeds (small envelopes or film canisters work well)

* Choose seeds with distinct characteristics so that differences will be readily apparent to kids. Choose at least two seeds that will give quick results—beans, carrots, radishes, lettuces, sunflowers, squash. You might also choose one kind that germinates very slowly or needs special care—apples or morning glories.

STUDENT HANDOUTS

- What Do I See?
- Choosing Seeds and Soil
- Directions for Starting Seeds
- How Did I Do?

CONCEPTS

- *experiment*—test under conditions that you control
- *germinate*—begin to grow or to sprout
- *seedling*—young plant grown from seed
- *observe*—watch carefully with attention to detail

Project Steps

This project asks students to experiment to see what conditions work best for growing seeds. They will germinate the seeds you've chosen in three different growing media—paper towels (so they can observe the process of germination), sand, and potting soil. They will observe how the seedlings grow and use the information they gather to decide what seeds and soil should be included in a seed-starting kit for kids. They will then make a Kids' Seed-Starter Kit, including instructions, supplies, and a decorative package for the kit.

Make sure you have all the supplies you need before you begin. Determine how many experiment stations you'll need to create for the number of students doing the project. To have every student in class experiment individually would involve a lot of materials, so it's usually best to set up only one or two experiments for all the students to observe.

Explain the project to the students and introduce the concepts they need to learn for this project. Talk with them about the standards of quality (see page 15) so they know how their work will be assessed.

Ask students to help you complete the following steps. Explain the reasoning behind each step as you go along.

Germination

Let students know that they are going to observe germination. They will put seeds on a damp paper towel inside a plastic bag and look at them each day to see what happens.

1. Fold a paper towel in half. Place three seeds of one kind on the towel, and then fold the towel to cover the seeds. Moisten the towel and seeds with water using an eyedropper or teaspoon, seal in a clear plastic bag, and set in a warm spot. Label the bag with masking tape, writing down the kind of seed and the date.

2. Repeat step 1 for each of the other types of seed.

Planting

Let the students know that while they watch the seeds in the paper towels to see when they begin to sprout, they also need to decide what kind of dirt to include in the kit. They will try to grow the seeds in sand and potting soil and see which works better.

3. Put one cup of **sand** in each of three small containers. Ask students to look at the sand and describe it.

4. Plant three seeds of the same kind in each container of sand. Label the containers with masking tape.

5. Ask students what else the seeds will need to grow. Let them know that seeds need to be moist to germinate, and that they'll need to

keep the dirt moist. Water the sand lightly (eight to twelve teaspoons).

6. Put one cup of **potting soil** in each of three small containers. Ask students to look at the potting soil and describe it. How is it like the sand? How is it different?

7. Plant three seeds of the same type in each container of potting soil. Label the containers with masking tape. Water the soil lightly (eight to twelve teaspoons).

Observation (What Do I See?)

8. Once the seeds have been planted, set aside a time every other day for students to make their observations. Explain that they will need to check the seeds (and later the plants) regularly. They will take turns observing the seeds—looking closely at them to see what happens—and recording their observations on the "What Do I See?" log (page 12). (You may want students to say what they see while you record their observations on the form, or you may ask them to draw what they see.) You can ask one student to check the paper towel, one the sand, and one the potting soil.

9. Explain that what they see happening to the seeds in the towels is also happening to the seeds planted in the sand and soil. At first, they will notice more activity in the paper towels as the seeds germinate. Later, as the seedlings emerge from the sand and soil, their focus will shift.

10. Students should check the seeds every other day. After observing the seeds, students can use an eyedropper or teaspoon to moisten the towels, sand, and soil.

11. After all of the seeds have been checked, ask students to compare their observations for each type of seed. Is one kind germinating faster than the others? Do they see any differences in the plants growing in sand from the ones in potting soil? Remind the class that later they will decide which kind of seed and which type of dirt is the best choice for their seed-starter kits. They must be able to explain why their choice is the best.

12. Continue observing for at least a week after the first plants emerge from the soil in one of the containers. As the days pass, the difference between the plants growing in each soil type will become more obvious.

Creating a Kids' Seed-Starter Kit

Once students have observed the seedlings and collected enough data, they can decide which seeds and which growing medium to include in their Kids' Seed-Starter Kit.

13. Distribute the "Choosing Seeds and Soil" handout (see page 13) to every child. Ask students to think about the three kinds of seeds. Which kind sprouted first? Which seed do they think is the most interesting to grow? Ask students to choose which kind of seeds to include in the kit and to explain the reasons for their choices. (Students with less-developed writing skills may dictate their answers.)

14. Talk about the dirt. Did the plants seem to grow better in the sand or the potting soil? What were the differences. Let students decide whether to include sand or soil in the kit and ask them to explain why. (Students with less-developed writing skills may dictate their answers.)

15. Guide students in writing a simple set of instructions for starting seeds. Use the "Directions for Starting Seeds" handout (see page 14). (Students with less-developed writing skills may dictate their answers.)

16. Talk about how to design a package for the Kids' Seed-Starter Kit. How will all of the materials go together so that they could be sold in a store? What kind of a container will hold the materials? What will the package contain?

17. Guide students in creating a complete package that includes seeds, soil, containers for planting seeds, paper towels, and pipettes. They should also include their final directions for starting seeds, and drawings to show what the seeds will look like when they germinate and grow. Provide materials so that students can create their final package (see list on page 9). Remind them that their package should have its name (The Kids' Seed-Starter Kit) prominently diplayed.

Extension Ideas

Let students experiment with other variables that might affect how well the seeds germinate and grow. For example, do seeds need light to germinate? Do the plants need light to grow? How much water do plants need to grow?

Let students observe the parts of a seedling under a magnifying glass or set up a microscope so students can view one of the seedlings from the paper towel under high magnification.

Notes

_____

_____

_____

_____

Name _____ Date _____

What Do I See?

What are the seeds in?	☐ paper towel	☐ sand	☐ soil

Seed #1 _____   **What do I see?**

Seed #2 _____   **What do I see?**

Seed #3 _____   **What do I see?**

Name _____ Date _____

KIDS' SEED-STARTER KIT
Choosing Seeds and Soil

Seeds

What kind of seeds will you put in the Kids' Seed-Starter Kit?

_____

Why are these seeds the best choice?

_____

_____

_____

Soil

What kind of soil will you put in the Kids' Seed-Starter Kit?

_____

Why is this soil the best choice?

_____

_____

_____

Name _____ Date _____

Directions for Starting Seeds

Write directions for using the seed kit in the box below.
Number each step. These directions will be put in the kit.

Here's How to Use the Kids' Seed-Starter Kit:

_____
_____
_____
_____
_____
_____
_____
_____
_____
_____
_____
_____
_____
_____
_____
_____

soil   seeds   tub   water   light   grow   germinate

Kids' Seed-Starter Kit: Standards of Quality

TASK	QUALITY STANDARD
1. Start seeds.	Help plant seeds in folded paper towels and in containers of sand and potting soil.
2. Keep seeds moist.	Use a spoon, an eyedropper, or a pipette to water the paper towels and containers as needed.
3. Observe the seeds on schedule and record observations.	Fill out a "What Do I See?" sheet as scheduled. Student drawings represent their best artistic efforts and show what the seeds in the paper towels and the seedlings in each container look like. Students can explain clearly what each drawing shows.
4. Decide which type of seed would be best to include in the seed-starter kit.	Identify one type of seed as being best suited for the kit and offer at least two carefully considered, sensible reasons for making that choice.
5. Decide which type of soil would be best to include in the seed-starter kit.	Identify one type of soil as being best suited for the kit and offer at least two carefully considered, sensible reasons for making that choice.
6. Write a set of directions that children could follow if they were to use the seed-starter kit.	Write out simple steps for starting seeds in paper towels and a container filled with soil. The steps are in proper sequence, neatly written, and easy to follow; they accurately describe how to start seeds and observe them as they germinate and grow.
7. Produce a Kids' Seed-Starter Kit.	Design a package that contains all of the necessary materials for a child to start seeds and observe them as they grow. The package contains soil, seeds, a paper towel, a paper cup, an eyedropper or pipette, directions, and drawings that show what the seeds will look like when they germinate and grow. The package is neat, orderly, and attractive. It has the product's name prominently displayed.

Name _____ Date _____

![logo] **KIDS' SEED-STARTER KIT**
How Did I Do?

Put a ✓ after each goal that was met.

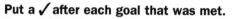

	STUDENT	TEACHER

I Used These Skills:
I followed directions. . . . .
I watered the seeds carefully. . . . .
I used my best art skills. . . . .
I used my best writing skills. . . . .
I worked well with others. . . . .

I Made These Things:
I started seeds in paper towels. . . . .
I started seeds in sand and soil. . . . .
I made drawings of my observations. . . . .
I wrote directions for starting seeds. . . . .
I designed a Kids' Seed-Starter Kit package. . . . .

I Learned These Things:
I know what a growing seed looks like. . . . .
I know there are different kinds of soil. . . . .
I know how to start seeds. . . . .
I chose the best seeds for kids to start. . . . .
I chose the best soil for growing seeds. . . . .
I know how to experiment. . . . .
I know how to observe. . . . .

Comments: _____

_____

_____

_____

_____

This Place Is a Zoo!

Intermediate Level

Every year millions of people visit zoos to marvel at the variety of animals that roam the earth. Almost every child at one time or another dreams of working in a zoo or going on safari to observe animals in their native environment. For this project, students assume the role of wildlife experts who design educational materials for animal exhibits.

During the project students will:

1. Study one type of natural habitat.

2. Study an animal that lives in that habitat.

3. Conduct research on that animal.

4. Design a sign for the exhibit.

5. Create at least one poster about the animal.

6. Draw a picture of the animal in its natural habitat.

7. Label a map to show where the animal comes from or lives naturally.

8. Develop a model of the animal exhibit (optional).

MATERIALS

- reference materials for conducting research on animals and habitats

- poster board or art paper for exhibit signs

- poster board or art paper for informative posters

- poster board or art paper for drawings of animals

- paints, markers, crayons, or other colored writing materials

STUDENT HANDOUTS

- Assignment Sheet
- Making an Exhibit Sign
- World Map
- Making an Exhibit Poster
- How Did I Do?

CONCEPTS

- *habitat*—the environment or place where an animal usually lives

- *classification*—scientific grouping of animals and plants based on their characteristics and relationship to each other

- *adaptations*—features that help animals or plants survive in their environment

- *predator*—an animal that eats another animal

- *prey*—an animal that is eaten by another animal

CONCEPTS continued. . .

- *food chain*—the relationship between predators and prey

- *carnivore*—an animal that eats other animals

- *omnivore*—an animal that eats other animals and plants

- *herbivore*—an animal that eats only plants

- *range*—geographic region in which an animal normally lives

Project Steps

1. Introduce the project scenario to the students: "You are a wildlife expert who works for a zoo. Your job is to help zoo visitors learn more about the animals they see by creating materials for a zoo exhibit." Hand out the "Assignment Sheet" and read through it with them. Discuss any concepts that may be unfamiliar to them. Be sure to talk about their responsibilities and expectations (see page 25).

2. Explain that the zoo where they work is organized by natural habitats; for example, all of the desert animal exhibits in the zoo are grouped in an area called "Animals of the Desert." Let each student choose a habitat from the list below:

- jungle or rainforest
- polar region
- plains/grasslands
- freshwater lake or river
- forest or woods
- desert
- mountain
- ocean
- swamp or pond
- seashore

3. Each student becomes an "expert" on one species of wildlife found in his or her chosen habitat. Students can choose which animal they'd like to study. Direct students to resource materials to determine what animals might live in the habitat they've selected (or to find out what habitat their favorite animal lives in). Distribute the "Making an Exhibit Sign" (see page 21) and the "Making an Exhibit Poster" (see page 23) handouts to guide students in gathering facts for their exhibit. Discuss the process with students and be available to answer questions.

4. Distribute outline maps of the world so students can color in where their animals live in nature.

5. Provide art materials for students to make their final exhibit signs and posters. The handouts they completed can guide them in making sure they have all the information they need for their exhibit.

6. Display the finished exhibit materials in your classroom or hallway. Allow students to present what they've learned about their animals to the rest of the class.

Extension Idea

Let students create a model or diorama of the animal in its exhibit or in its natural habitat.

Notes

_____

_____

_____

_____

_____

_____

_____

_____

_____

_____

_____

_____

_____

_____

_____

_____

_____

_____

Name _____ Date _____

THIS PLACE IS A ZOO!
Assignment Sheet

You are a wildlife expert who works for a zoo. Your job is to help zoo visitors learn about the animals they see. Read the assignment below, and then use the sign and poster handouts to make materials for a zoo exhibit.

1. Choose the habitat you'd like to study:

- jungle or rainforest
- polar region
- plains/grasslands
- freshwater lake or river
- forest or woods
- desert
- mountain
- ocean
- swamp or pond
- seashore

2. After researching your habitat, choose an animal to study that lives in the habitat.

I will study the _____

3. Make a sign for the animal exhibit (the "Making an Exhibit Sign" handout will guide you). The sign should include:

- the name of the animal in large letters
- the animal's habitat in the wild
- the animal's classification (bird, mammal, fish, insect, reptile, amphibian, etc.)
- the animal's diet (is it a carnivore, herbivore, or omnivore?)
- the continent where the animal lives
- at least two other interesting facts

4. Color an outline map to show where the animal you are studying lives in the wild. Be as accurate as possible.

5. Make one large poster or several small posters for the animal exhibit. "Making an Exhibit Poster" handouts will guide you in recording information. You will:

- Describe at least three adaptations, or body features (teeth, feet, eyes, ears, color, shape, size, etc.), that help the animal survive in its natural habitat.

- Create a food chain that has at least four links, including the sun.

- Describe your animal's body covering, heating system (is it warm-blooded or cold-blooded?), type of reproduction, and breathing system.

- Present at least five other interesting facts that you find in your research.

6. Draw a picture of the animal in its natural habitat. Show what the animal looks like and the surroundings it lives in. You may include this illustration on your poster or display it separately.

7. Display or present your finished exhibit.

Name _____ Date _____

THIS PLACE IS A ZOO!
Making an Exhibit Sign

Habitat _____ Animal _____

1. This animal is classified as: (choose one)

☐ a fish
☐ an amphibian
☐ a reptile
☐ a bird
☐ a mammal
☐ an insect
☐ other_____

2. This animal eats: (choose one)

☐ only meat, which means it is a *carnivore*
☐ only plants, which means it is an *herbivore*
☐ both plants and meat, which means it is an *omnivore*

3. This animal lives mostly on the continent of _____.

4. Here are some other facts about this animal that I will put on the sign:

_____

_____

_____

_____

_____

_____

Name _____ Date _____

THIS PLACE IS A ZOO!

World Map

Here is where the _____ lives in the wild.

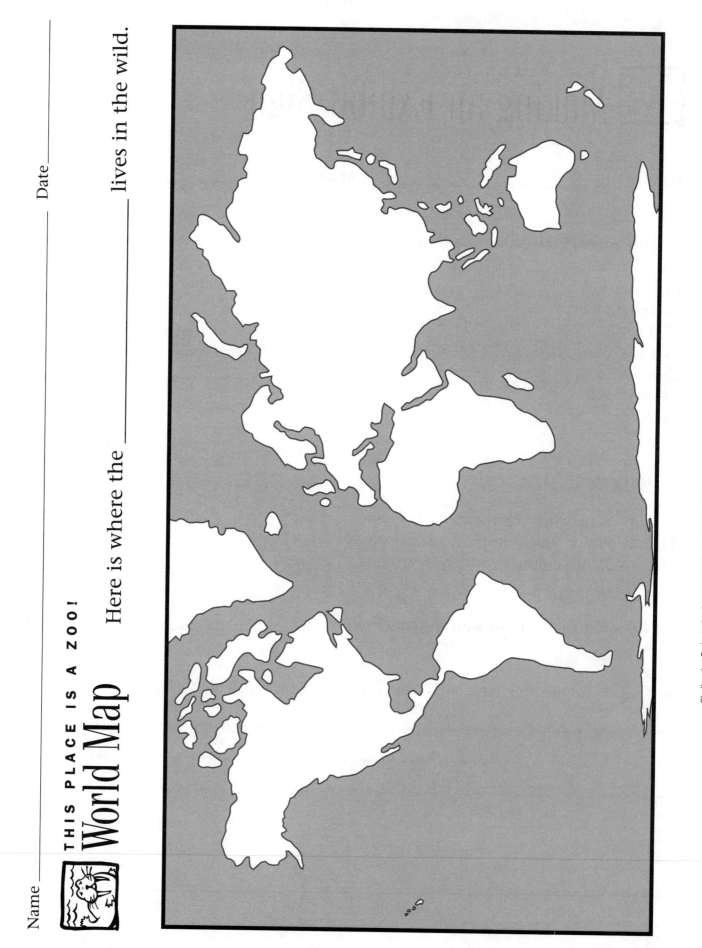

Challenging Projects for Creative Minds © 1999 by Phil Schlemmer and Dori Schlemmer. Free Spirit Publishing Inc.
Minneapolis, MN 1-800-735-7323

Name _____ Date _____

THIS PLACE IS A ZOO!
Making an Exhibit Poster

Habitat _____ Animal _____

1. All animals have adaptations, or special body features, that help them survive in the wild. For example, buffalo have flat teeth for crushing and grinding food before swallowing; male cardinals have bright feathers that help them attract a mate. Describe three of your animal's adaptations below and include these on your poster. This animal has:

DESCRIPTION OF BODY PART	PURPOSE
1.	
2.	
3.	

2. All animals are also part of a food chain. Show how your animal fits into a simple food chain, starting with the sun. For example: sun ➡ oak tree ➡ squirrel ➡ eagle

Here is a food chain for my poster:

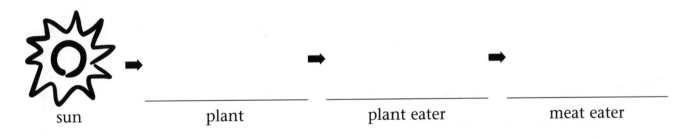

sun　　　　　　　plant　　　　　　plant eater　　　　　meat eater

3. This animal has four important characteristics that I will put on my poster:

Body Covering
☐ hair or fur
☐ feathers
☐ dry scales
☐ wet, slimy scales
☐ moist skin
☐ outside skeleton

Breathing System
☐ lungs only
☐ gills and lungs
☐ gills only
☐ body openings

Heating System
☐ cold-blooded
(can't make its own heat)
☐ warm-blooded
(makes its own heat)

Reproduction
☐ thin, moist eggs
☐ leathery eggs
☐ hard, brittle eggs
☐ born alive

Here are five other interesting facts about this animal that I will include on my poster:

Fact 1: _____

_____

_____

_____

Fact 2: _____

_____

_____

_____

Fact 3: _____

_____

_____

_____

Fact 4: _____

_____

_____

_____

Fact 5: _____

_____

_____

_____

This Place Is a Zoo: Standards of Quality

TASK	QUALITY STANDARD
1. Choose a topic.	Select a habitat and identify an animal that lives in that habitat.
2. Classify the animal.	Correctly identify it as a fish, amphibian, reptile, bird, mammal, insect, or other.
3. Identify the animal's type of diet.	Determine whether the animal is a carnivore, herbivore, or omnivore.
4. Locate the animal's natural habitat geographically.	Carefully and accurately mark the animal's natural habitat on a world map.
5. Identify adaptations.	Accurately describe at least three adaptations that help the animal survive in the wild.
6. Describe a food chain.	Correctly determine how the animal fits into a food chain with at least four links. The food chain is drawn as a flow of energy, beginning with the sun.
7. Define four main characteristics that can be used to classify the animal.	Correctly define the animal's characteristics in each of four categories: body covering, breathing system, heating system, and type of reproduction.
8. Conduct research.	Apply research skills to verify that enough information is available and to find useful facts about the animal.
9. Create a drawing of the animal.	Use their best artistic skills to make a drawing of the animal that is accurate in detail, setting, and color.
10. Design a sign for the exhibit.	Produce a sign that is neat, clear, and informative. It includes the animal's name, habitat, classification, diet type, natural range (where it lives in the wild), and other information.
11. Design a poster or set of posters.	Produce a poster that is neat, clear, and informative and includes three adaptations, a four-link food chain, classification characteristics, and five additional interesting facts.

Name _____ Date _____

THIS PLACE IS A ZOO!
How Did I Do?

	STUDENT			TEACHER		
	I DID BETTER THAN I EXPECTED	I DID AS WELL AS I EXPECTED	I NEED MORE TIME	STUDENT DID BETTER THAN I EXPECTED	STUDENT MET MY EXPECTATIONS	STUDENT NEEDS MORE TIME

I Used These Skills:

I followed directions. ....

I chose a good topic (plenty of information). ....

I used my best art skills. ....

I used my best writing skills. ....

I found information about my animal. ....

I wrote information on my handouts. ....

I carefully designed a sign. ....

I carefully designed a poster. ....

I worked well with others. ....

I finished tasks on time. ....

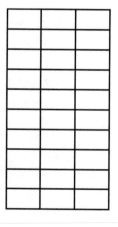

I Made These Things:

I produced a sign for the animal exhibit. ....

I made a poster for the animal exhibit. ....

I created a drawing of the animal. ....

I marked a world map to show habitat. ....

I described three adaptations in writing. ....

I drew a food chain with four links. ....

I Learned These Things:

I know what class the animal belongs to. ....

I know some adaptations of the animal. ....

I know how to describe adaptations. ....

I can draw a food chain for the animal. ....

I know where the animal comes from. ....

I know what the animal eats. ....

I know the terms carnivore, herbivore, and omnivore. ....

I know what the animal looks like. ....

I know the animal's characteristics. ....

I know other facts from research. ....

Comments: _____

_____

_____

The Animal Inventor

Advanced Level

In this project, students demonstrate what they know about animals by applying their knowledge to invent new animals. Students act as zoological advisers who create imaginary animals for a science fiction movie. In the script, scientists have discovered a mysterious planet in our solar system—one with a climate and geology just like Earth's. Because the sun is always directly between Earth and this planet, nobody has ever known of its existence. Explorers discover the planet and encounter its animal inhabitants.

The movie's director has asked zoological experts to create animals for the movie. She's asked that the new animals belong to the same classes as Earth animals but be different from any creature found on our planet. In other words, the new planet has mammals, birds, reptiles, insects, crustaceans, and arachnids—but they are like no animals ever seen!

During the project students will:

1. Classify and name two animals.

2. Describe at least three characteristics that are used to classify the animals. (For example, what are three characteristics that tell us that a koala is a mammal?)

3. Identify a predator-prey relationship between the two animals.

4. Describe the animals' habitat.

5. Explain what each animal needs for survival.

6. Describe at least four important adaptations, or body features, of the animals.

7. Make posters displaying the information on their animals.

MATERIALS

- reference materials
- poster board or art paper
- paint, markers, crayons, or other drawing materials

STUDENT HANDOUTS

- Assignment Sheet
- Predators
- Prey
- Animal Adaptations
- How Did I Do?

CONCEPTS

- *habitat*—the environment or place where an animal usually lives

- *classification*—scientific grouping of animals and plants based on their characteristics and relationship to each other

- *adaptations*—features that help animals or plants survive in their environment

- *predator*—an animal that eats another animal

- *prey*—an animal that is eaten by another animal

- *food chain*—the relationship between predators and prey

- *carnivore*—an animal that eats other animals

- *omnivore*—an animal that eats other animals and plants

- *herbivore*—an animal that eats only plants

Project Steps

1. Give students the "Assignment Sheet," (see page 30) and discuss the project's requirements and expectations (see page 34). Read through the scenario, and review the concepts with students before they begin their projects.

2. Give students the "Predators" handout (see page 31) to guide their decisions and record information about the first of two imaginary animals. Check their work and make comments or suggestions.

3. Give students the "Prey" handout (see page 32) to guide them in making decisions and recording information about the second animal they will invent. Collect the "Prey" handouts to check their work and make comments or suggestions.

4. Give students the "Animal Adaptations" handout (see page 33). This sheet asks students to describe adaptations for each of the animals they are inventing. Check the adaptation handouts and make comments or suggestions.

5. Discuss the next steps with the students. They will create posters that include all of the information from the handouts plus detailed drawings of the animals.

6. Supply poster board or art paper and instruct students to develop posters of the animals they have invented, following the guidelines described on the "Assignment Sheet." Recommend that students sketch a rough draft of each poster to be certain of layout, spacing, and organization before they produce a finished poster.

7. Give students an opportunity to display their posters and present their animals to the rest of the class.

Extension Ideas

Let students name the planet, make maps to show its geography, write adventure stories about exploring it, write a scene for the movie—featuring the animals they've invented.

Several students can work together to develop an extended food chain using all of their animals. The project can be made even more challenging by asking students to make a food web, showing more complex relationships between animals and their foods. Hint: only one or two animals should be designated as top predators; the other carnivores should be intermediate predators, meaning that they don't hunt the top predators. There should also be herbivores.

Notes

_____
_____
_____
_____
_____
_____
_____
_____
_____
_____
_____
_____
_____
_____
_____
_____
_____
_____

Name _____ Date _____

THE ANIMAL INVENTOR
Assignment Sheet

You are a zoologist who has been hired by a movie director to help with a film. The action takes place on a newly discovered planet in our solar system. Because the sun is always directly between Earth and this planet, nobody has ever seen it or known of its existence before now. When a space team goes to investigate, they discover a world very much like Earth: it's the same size, same distance from the sun, same atmosphere, same climate, plenty of water, and lots of animal life.

You've been hired to invent the animals that live on the planet. The director will use your ideas to make models and computer-animated creatures for the movie.

1. You'll invent two animals for the movie project. Three handouts will help you develop descriptions of your animals.

2. Turn each handout in when it is finished. Use your teacher's comments to make any necessary changes.

3. Design a poster for each animal that you invent. Sketch out a first draft of each poster before you make your final drawings. A draft allows you to experiment with layout, use of space, and organization. You'll be surprised at how much better your work turns out when you take the time to do a first draft and make improvements.

For each poster you create:

• Name the animal you've invented.

• Make a detailed drawing of the animal.

• Tell what class the animal belongs to (mammal, bird, reptile, amphibian, etc.) and explain how you can tell the animal belongs to that class. Your two animals may not belong to the same class. Each animal must be in a class by itself!

• Describe the animal's habitat.

• Explain what the animal needs to survive in its environment.

• Identify the animal as a predator or prey animal. One of your animals will be a predator and the other will be its prey. This means they must live close to each other. Keep this in mind as you describe each animal's habitat.

• Describe at least two body features, or adaptations, that help the animal either hunt for food or escape from a predator.

• Describe at least two other important adaptations that help the animal live in its habitat.

4. Display your posters and be prepared to discuss the animals you've created.

Name _____ Date _____

THE ANIMAL INVENTOR
Predators

My predator animal is called _____

What class does this animal belong to?

☐ Amphibian   ☐ Cephalopod   ☐ Insect
☐ Arachnid   ☐ Crustacean   ☐ Mammal
☐ Bird   ☐ Fish   ☐ Reptile

What three characteristics does this animal have that put it in this class?

1. _____

2. _____

3. _____

Describe the animal's natural habitat (remember, it must live close to the other animal you invent).

Climate:

☐ Polar
☐ Temperate
☐ Tropical

Environment:

☐ Desert   ☐ Mountain
☐ Forest   ☐ Ocean
☐ Grassland   ☐ River
☐ Jungle   ☐ Other:
☐ Lake   _____

Habitat:

☐ Arboreal (tree dwelling)
☐ Aquatic (water dwelling)
☐ Terrestrial (land dwelling)

Other Details:

_____

_____

Identify three basic needs that this animal faces in its habitat and explain how it meets those needs:

	Basic Need	**How It Is Met**
1.	_____	_____
2.	_____	_____
3.	_____	_____

Name _____ Date _____

THE ANIMAL INVENTOR
Prey

My prey animal is called _____

What class does this animal belong to?

☐ Amphibian   ☐ Cephalopod   ☐ Insect
☐ Arachnid   ☐ Crustacean   ☐ Mammal
☐ Bird   ☐ Fish   ☐ Reptile

What three characteristics does this animal have that put it in this class?

1. _____

2. _____

3. _____

Describe the animal's natural habitat (remember, it must live close to the other animal you invent).

Climate:

☐ Polar
☐ Temperate
☐ Tropical

Environment:

☐ Desert   ☐ Mountain
☐ Forest   ☐ Ocean
☐ Grassland   ☐ River
☐ Jungle   ☐ Other:
☐ Lake   _____

Habitat:

☐ Arboreal (tree dwelling)
☐ Aquatic (water dwelling)
☐ Terrestrial (land dwelling)

Other Details:

_____

_____

Identify three basic needs that this animal faces in its habitat and explain how it meets those needs:

Basic Need	How It Is Met
1. _____	_____
2. _____	_____
3. _____	_____

Name _____ Date _____

THE ANIMAL INVENTOR
Animal Adaptations

PREDATOR ANIMAL'S NAME: _____

Describe two adaptations that help the animal hunt its food.

1. _____

_____

2. _____

_____

Describe two adaptations that help the animal survive in its habitat.

1. _____

_____

2. _____

_____

PREY ANIMAL'S NAME: _____

Describe two adaptations that help the animal escape from a predator.

1. _____

_____

2. _____

_____

Describe two adaptations that help the animal survive in its habitat.

1. _____

_____

2. _____

_____

The Animal Inventor: Standards of Quality

TASK	QUALITY STANDARD
1. Invent two animals.	Carefully and completely follow guidelines to develop the defining characteristics for two imaginary animals.
2. Produce a poster for each animal.	Create a rough draft and final poster for each animal. The final poster displays all of the information from the handouts in an organized, informative fashion.
3. Create a drawing of each animal.	Make a detailed drawing of each animal. The drawing clearly shows what the animal looks like and illustrates information from handouts.
4. Classify each animal.	Identify each animal's class and accurately describe three characteristics that put the animal in that class.
5. Describe each animal's habitat.	Define each animal's habitat by its climate, environment, and dwelling, and provide additional details. Both animals live near each other.
6. Identify each animal as a predator or as a prey animal.	Create a two-animal food chain by designing one animal to be a predator that hunts and eats the other.
7. Describe adaptations that help each animal either find food or escape predators.	The student invents at least two carefully considered predator/prey adaptations for each animal and describes them fully.
8. Describe adaptations that help each animal live in its habitat.	Invent at least two carefully considered habitat-related adaptations for each animal and describe them fully.
9. Explain what each animal needs for survival and how those needs are met.	Identify at least three basic needs that each animal has and explain how those needs are met. The three most basic needs are water, food, and shelter. The student may focus on these, or identify others.

Name _____ Date _____

THE ANIMAL INVENTOR
How Did I Do?

SELF TEACHER

I Used These Skills:

I followed directions carefully and fully. ....

I used my creativity and imagination to invent two animals. ....

I applied my best art skills to draw two imaginary animals. ....

I used organization skills to design and lay out two posters. ....

I conducted research to learn about classifying animals. ....

I used my best writing skills. ....

I finished tasks on time. ....

I Made These Things:

I created two detailed imaginary animal posters showing:

● each animal's class (each animal a different class). ....

● each animal's habitat (each animal the same habitat). ....

● each animal's place in the food chain (predator/prey). ....

● two predator/prey adaptations for each animal. ....

● two habitat survival adaptations. ....

● three basic needs for each animal and how they are met. ....

I Learned These Things:

I learned about how animals are classified. ....

I learned about animal habitats and adaptations. ....

I learned about animal predator-prey relationships. ....

I learned about the basic needs of animals. ....

I learned to use my imagination to show what I know. ....

Comments: _____

_____

_____

_____

_____

_____

PART 2

Numbers & Measurement

The School Sign Company
Beginning Level

This project introduces students to the ideas of measurement and record keeping. Students act as sign makers for the School Sign Company. They have been hired to create signs telling how far it is from one point to another in the room and in the school. Students can choose their own measuring instruments (such as scarves or broom handles) or you can supply standard measuring instruments if your curriculum emphasizes standard measurement.

During the project students will:

1. Carefully measure and record distances in the room and in the school.

2. Make signs that tell how far it is to various destinations in the room and around the school.

3. Display their signs in appropriate places in the room and in the school.

4. Contribute to a chart that lists all the distances students have measured.

MATERIALS

- instruments for measuring distances in the classroom (for example, unsharpened pencils, 1-foot pieces of yarn or twine)

- instruments for measuring distances in the school building (for example, dowel rods, shoelaces, brooms, winter scarves)

- markers, crayons, or other art materials

- Distance Data Chart (copied onto an overhead)

STUDENT HANDOUTS

- Record What You Measure (one for each pair of students)

- "From Here It Is . . ." template

- How Did I Do?

CONCEPTS

- *linear measurement*—measuring distance or length in a straight line

- *record keeping*—keeping track of facts and information

- *teamwork*—working together with other people to meet a goal

Project Steps

1. Introduce the concept of linear measurement, or measuring distance on a straight line. Find out what students already know about measuring distances or length through class discussion. Tell them that for this project they will work with a partner to measure how far it is from one place to another within the classroom and within the school. Then they will make signs to show the distance between the two places. Show students the measuring instruments you've collected.

2. Pair students up to work as partners, and let them practice measuring before they begin the project. Students need to master two basic skills to get accurate measurements, so you'll want to model the method. Or ask for volunteers to help: (a) carefully place the measuring instrument, mark the end with a finger, move the instrument in a straight line to the other side of the finger, and continue this process until reaching the destination; and (b) keep accurate count of how many times the instrument is moved.

3. Guide students in choosing distances to measure both in the room and in the school (for example, the distance between the pencil sharpener and the aquarium or the classroom and the music room). If you prefer, you can select the distances for students to measure in advance. For each pair of students working on the project, list the beginning point and end point for two distances on the handout "Record What You Measure."

4. Distribute to each pair of students a "Record What You Measure" handout with their locations written in. Take plenty of time to explain the data sheet and practice using it before letting students work on their own.

5. Have partners make their measurements, choosing the measuring instruments that you've provided. Accurate measurement and correct record keeping are important outcomes of this activity, so monitor the pairs as necessary and offer feedback.

6. Once students have completed their measurements and gathered their data, instruct student pairs in making signs using their measurements. Distribute the "From Here It Is . . ." template for students to fill out and decorate. Remind them to include their units of distance on their signs. Ask students to display a sign at each beginning point to show how far it is to the end point. They can draw an arrow on the sign showing the correct direction.

7. Ask students to report the results of their measurements to the class. Display the results on the "Distance Data Chart." This provides a record of everyone's work. Allow class discussion to help students process the information.

Extension Ideas

Develop a list of unusual distances and let students create colorful signs with pictures to place around the classroom or school. Provide resources for kids to look up the distances. For example, from the classroom to the sun and the moon; from the classroom to Paris, Beijing, Cairo, and other world capitals; from the bottom of the teacher's feet to the top of his or her head.

You can also talk about other kinds of measurement: time, weight, speed, volume, etc.

Notes

Name _____ Date _____

THE SCHOOL SIGN COMPANY
Record What You Measure

In the Classroom	**In the School**
Begin: _____	Begin: _____
_____	_____
_____	_____
End: _____	End: _____
_____	_____
_____	_____
Make a mark in this box every time you measure one unit (ᵗᴴᴸ I).	Make a mark in this box every time you measure one unit (ᵗᴴᴸ I).
Results	**Results**
Total Distance: _____	Total Distance: _____
Units: _____	Units: _____

Name _____ Date _____

THE SCHOOL SIGN COMPANY
Distance Data Chart

Classroom Distances

Measuring Partners	Beginning Point	Ending Point	Distance	Units
and				
and				
and				
and				
and				
and				

School Distances

Measuring Partners	Beginning Point	Ending Point	Distance	Units
and				
and				
and				
and				
and				
and				

From here it is

Distance _____

to _____

Units _____

Measured by: _____ and _____

The School Sign Company: Standards of Quality

TASK	QUALITY STANDARD
1. Measure a distance in the classroom.	Work with a partner to measure accurately the distance between two points in the classroom, using a predetermined unit of measure.
2. Measure a distance in the school.	Work with a partner to measure accurately the distance between two points in the school, using a predetermined unit of measure.
3. Record measurements on a data sheet.	Record each measurement of one unit on a data sheet and then write the correct total distance and the units used on the sheet. Two sets of data are recorded: one for a classroom distance and one for a school distance.
4. Produce a classroom sign.	Complete a sign that tells how far it is from one given point in the room to another given point. The sign is properly positioned in the room and includes an accurate distance, the correct units, the destination, the names of the students who worked together, and an arrow pointing in the right direction.
5. Produce a school sign.	Complete a sign that tells how far it is from one given place in the school to another given point. The sign is properly positioned in the school and includes an accurate distance, the correct units, the destination, the names of the students who worked together, and an arrow pointing in the right direction.
6. Contribute to a class data chart of all of the measurements made during the project.	Supply classroom and school measurement data when called upon so that the teacher can record it on a class data chart. This involves reporting who the partners were, identifying the beginning and ending points of each measurement, giving the measurement, and telling what units were used.

Name _____ Date _____

THE SCHOOL SIGN COMPANY
How Did I Do?

Put a ✓ after each goal that was met.

	STUDENT	TEACHER
	☺	☺

I Used These Skills:

I followed directions. ....

I used my best measuring skills. ....

I used my best writing skills. ....

I cooperated with my partner. ....

I wrote information correctly. ....

I measured and recorded a classroom distance. ....

I measured and recorded a school distance. ....

I Made These Things:

I made a classroom measurement sign. ....

I made a school measurement sign. ....

I helped make a class data chart. ....

I Learned These Things:

I can measure between two points. ....

I can write measurements with units. ....

I can use arrows to show direction. ....

I can report data accurately. ....

Comments: _____

_____

_____

_____

_____

_____

School Census Bureau

Intermediate Level

Combining written questions, math calculations, and visual representations of numbers, survey research offers an excellent way for students to work across the curriculum. In this project, students act as data collectors for the school census bureau. Teams of students send "Census Bureau Questionnaires" to teachers in other classrooms to collect data about the students in each room. Then they make wall graphs to show their findings. (Before you send your students to collect information from other teachers, please ask your colleagues whether they're willing to help.)

During the project each team of three to five students will:

1. Prepare a "Census Bureau Questionnaire" to send to teachers from one grade.

2. Complete a "Census Data Chart" for the grade being studied.

3. Measure and cut paper strips to scale to represent collected data.

4. Help design and produce wall graphs that include data from each team.

MATERIALS

- adding machine paper rolls for wall graphs (one roll per group)
- rulers

STUDENT HANDOUTS

- Assignment Sheet
- Census Bureau Questionnaire (one for each classroom teacher in your school)
- Census Data Chart (one for each team of students)
- How Did I Do?

CONCEPTS

- *census*—a population count
- *survey*—a set of questions used to gather information from many people
- *bar graph*—a chart that uses thick lines to show differences in amounts

Project Steps

1. Introduce the project to the students. Distribute the "Assignment Sheet" (see page 49) and go through it with them, discussing the purpose of a census and taking a survey. Find out what students already know about a census and the kind of information that is gathered. What is that information used for? Talk about the project requirements and discuss the standards of quality (see page 52) so they will know what to expect.

2. Divide the class into teams. Create one team for each grade in your school. For example, if your building serves kids in grades K to 5, you should have six School Census Bureau teams. Assign each team a grade level to survey.

3. Ask each team to prepare a "Census Bureau Questionnaire" (see page 50) to distribute to the teachers in their assigned grade level. The survey lists two questions, but the class should add more questions of their own. For example:

- How many students can speak a second language?
- How many students have moved in the past year?

All teams must agree on the additional Census Bureau questions so that the entire school can answer the same questions.

Guide students in developing a set of questions that will help them get at other census data as well. For example, the standard questions on the "Census Bureau Questionnaire" ask for the total number of students in the class and the number of girls in the class. Using the results of these two questions, students can calculate the number of boys in the class.

4. After students have written out their surveys, deliver the "Census Bureau Questionnaires" to the appropriate teachers in the building and ask them to provide data for your class.

5. Introduce the concept of bar graphs to students. Show samples, and discuss how to make a bar graph. Model how to construct a simple wall graph that students can refer to later when they make their own. For example, create a graph to show the number of students in your room who have a pet and the number who don't, using a scale of 1 student = 1 inch.

Once students have the results of their survey, guide them in following the steps on the "Assignment Sheet" to collect and record the data, as well as organize the information. After recording their results on a "Census Data

Chart," (see page 51) each team will represent the data it collects by producing paper strips measured to scale (1 student = 1 inch) to be used as bars on a wall graph.

6. Invite students to think about how they can make simple calculations to gain more data, without asking for additional information. For example, the questionnaire asks how many students are in the class and how many girls are in the class. Students can calculate how many boys are in the class by subtracting the number of girls from the total students. What other information could students get from their additional questions?

7. In a large group, develop wall graphs to display the information each team collected. Each team will provide the data it collected for each category and help create a bar graph to illustrate the data.

8. Discuss the results of the census with your class. Ask questions about the data to help students think about the information. For example, which class had the most students? Which class had the most boys? Did any of the information surprise them? What did they learn through this process?

Extension Ideas

Ask students about what other kinds of graphs they could make using their data. Talk about different kinds of graphs and how they show different types of information:

- Bar graphs make comparisons.
- Stacked bar graphs show the parts that contribute to the totals.
- Pie charts show relationships between the whole and its parts.

Notes

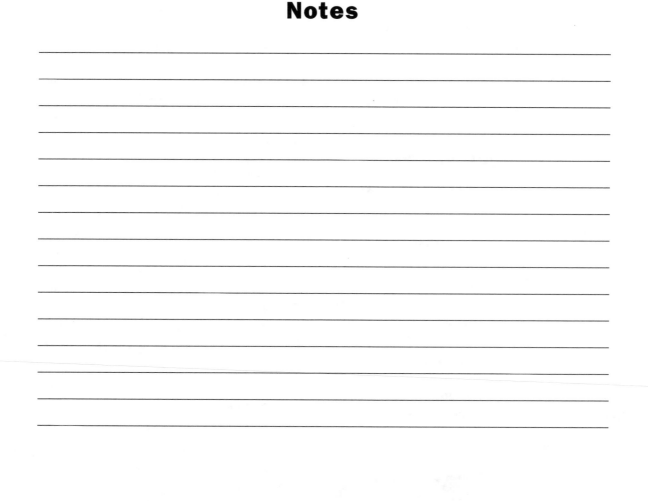

Name _____ Date _____

SCHOOL CENSUS BUREAU
Assignment Sheet

Census Team Members

_____   _____   _____

_____   _____   _____

A *census* is a survey that counts all the people in a population. The United States conducts a census every ten years, counting all the people that live in the country and gathering other specific data about them. You'll work in teams to conduct a census of all the students in the school.

Your team will survey one grade by sending a census questionnaire to the teachers of that grade. You will ask for data about the students in each teacher's class. Your team will share data with the other teams and help make wall graphs that show the results.

Read the assignment below.

1. Prepare a "Census Bureau Questionnaire" for each teacher in the grade your team is studying. (We will discuss how to do this in class.)

2. When you get the questionnaires back, write the information from them onto the "Census Data Chart." This is called "collecting and recording data." (We will discuss how to do this in class.)

3. Use the scale 1 student = 1 inch to determine how long your bars should be. If there are 25 students in a class, for example, then your bar should be 25 inches long. If there are 72 students in a grade, then your bar for the grade should be 72 inches long. Determine the length for each question you asked, and record it on your data sheet.

4. Measure and cut a paper strip for the first "Total" on your "Census Data Chart." Label it so that you remember what information it represents. For example, "There are 72 students in the fourth grade at our school." Write your team name on the back of each strip.

5. Repeat step 4 for each "Total" on your survey.

6. In a large-group discussion, talk about the project. What other information can you get from the data you collected?

7. What information from your school census is most important? Decide as a large group what information would be helpful to display in bar graphs. For example, you could create a graph showing the number of students in each grade or the number of girls in the school.

8. Help your class make wall bar graphs to show the data you collected. Be sure to talk about these things for each graph idea:

- What will the graph show? (What is the category?)
- How will the bars be arranged on the wall?
- How will the graph be labeled?

9. What did you learn by doing the census? Discuss the results in class.

Name _____ Date _____

SCHOOL CENSUS BUREAU

Census Bureau Questionnaire

Census Team Members

_____   _____   _____

_____   _____   _____

Class: _____

_____

To:

Teacher _____ Grade _____

We are doing a school census. Our team has been assigned to collect data about your class. Please answer the questions below and return this questionnaire to our teacher. Thank you very much for your help.

When we are done, you may come to our room to see the results of our work.

1. How many students are in your class?   _____

2. How many girls are in your class?   _____

3. _____

_____   _____

4. _____

_____   _____

5. _____

_____   _____

6. _____

_____   _____

Name _____ Date _____

SCHOOL CENSUS BUREAU

Census Data Chart for Grade _____

Record the data from the Census Bureau Questionnaires that you sent out.

QUESTION	TEACHER	TEACHER	TEACHER	TEACHER	TEACHER	TEACHER	TEACHER	TEACHER	TOTAL
1. How many students are in your class?									
2. How many girls are in your class?									
3.									
4.									
5.									
6.									

Challenging Projects for Creative Minds © 1999 by Phil Schlemmer and Dori Schlemmer. Free Spirit Publishing Inc.

School Census Bureau: Standards of Quality

TASK	QUALITY STANDARD
1. Work cooperatively in a small group.	Work effectively in a group: offer input, contribute to final products, accept others' ideas, show sufficient effort, and remain on task.
2. Complete at least one "Census Bureau Questionnaire" to send to a teacher.	Completely and properly fill out at least one questionnaire.
3. Transfer data from "Census Bureau Questionnaire" to a "Census Data Chart."	Neatly and accurately transfer data from questionnaires to the "Census Data Chart."
4. Calculate totals for an entire grade.	Calculate accurate totals for an entire grade by adding the numbers collected from other classrooms.
5. Use existing data to create additional data.	Use existing data to calculate new data; for example, knowing the total number of students and the number of girls, calculate the number of boys.
6. Calculate bar graph lengths for each "Total" on the "Census Data Chart."	Determine the appropriate bar length for each question and correctly record it on the "Census Data Chart."
7. Cut strips of paper to be used as bars on a wall graph.	Correctly measure bars using data from the "Census Data Chart" and carefully create bars of the proper length.
8. Label paper strips to show what they represent.	Label each bar for the graph with a clear and easily understood description of what it represents, using best writing skills.
9. Identify categories for bar graphs that will show data about the student population in the school.	Participate in class discussions to decide what categories of bar graphs to make from the data that is available.
10. Create bar graphs on the walls of the classroom.	Help develop bar graphs that correctly show school census data and analyze the information gathered.

Name _____ Date _____

 SCHOOL CENSUS BUREAU
How Did I Do?

	STUDENT			TEACHER		
	I DID BETTER THAN I EXPECTED	I DID AS WELL AS I EXPECTED	I NEED MORE TIME	STUDENT DID BETTER THAN I EXPECTED	STUDENT MET MY EXPECTATIONS	STUDENT NEEDS MORE TIME

I Used These Skills:

I followed directions.						
I worked well with others.						
I used my best writing skills.						
I used math skills to create new data.						
I measured bars for the graphs accurately.						
I carefully and neatly created bars for the graphs.						
I helped to develop wall graphs.						
I finished tasks on time.						

I Made These Things:

I helped create a "Census Bureau Questionnaire."						
I recorded data on a "Census Data Chart."						
I measured and created bars for graphs.						
I wrote labels for all my bars to tell what they show.						
I helped make wall graphs.						

I Learned These Things:

I know how to make bar graphs.						
I know how bar graphs are used.						
I know how to collect data.						
I know how to organize data.						
I can use math to create new data.						
I know about our school's population.						

Comments: _____

_____

_____

_____

_____

_____

Buying the Car of My Dreams

Advanced Level

Who couldn't use an early introduction to consumer math? Give your students a look at what it costs to drive off in the car of their dreams. In this project, students imagine that they're old enough to drive and that they've just landed a good-paying job. But they need a new car to get to work every day. A relative has agreed to finance a car by lending students the money to buy whatever car they wish. The students have agreed to repay the loan in annual payments of $6,000. This project works best if students have already studied percentages, graphing, and equations, although students who are strong in math may pick up the concepts easily.

During the project students will:

1. Select the car of their dreams.

2. Determine how much the car will cost them (including taxes, licensing, interest, and other charges).

3. Research interest rates at local banks and credit unions.

4. Calculate the principal and interest they will pay over the life of the loan.

5. Create a bar graph showing the relationships between interest, principal, and time.

MATERIALS

- resources for researching car prices, tax and license fees, and interest rates
- graph paper
- fine-tip colored markers or colored pencils
- calculators (optional)

STUDENT HANDOUTS

- Assignment Sheet
- Researching Principal and Interest
- Figuring the First Year's Costs
- Loan Payment Chart
- Principal and Interest Bar Graph
- How Did I Do?

CONCEPTS

- *principal*—the amount of money owed on a loan, not including interest
- *interest*—the price paid for borrowing money, usually expressed as a percentage
- *annual percentage rate (APR)*—a percentage that measures what it costs you to borrow money over a year

Project Steps

1. Introduce the project to the students. Distribute the "Assignment Sheet" (see page 57). Talk through each step and the concepts to be sure they understand annual percentage rate (APR) and that they can use the equation

P x R x T = I.
(Principal x Rate of interest x Time = Interest Owed)

2. Discuss the "Standards of Quality" (see page 63) to make sure students know what's expected of them. Answer any questions.

3. Hand out "Researching Principal and Interest" (see page 58). Discuss the research needed to determine the principal of the loan (the total cost of the car) and the interest rate (the best car loan rate students can discover).

Note: There's an upper limit to what students can spend on their car. If the annual interest they'd owe is $6,000 or more, students won't be able to repay the principal on the loan. Discuss this with students and determine the upper limit in class so students don't spend too much time on impossible dreams. Use this formula:

$6,000 ÷ R = maximum total cost
(R = Rate of interest)

Work out the problem using several different interest rates. This is a good way of showing students how interest rates can affect purchase decisions.

4. Direct students to record the information they find on the "Researching Principal and Interest" handout, based upon their research and initial calculations. As students complete the handout, check their work.

5. Return the "Researching Principal and Interest" handout and give students "Figuring the First Year's Costs" (see page 60). Hold a class discussion if necessary to help students figure out how to do the calculations. Ask students to calculate each cell on the chart and then hand it in to be checked.

6. Return the "Figuring the First Year's Costs" handout and give students the "Loan Payment Chart" (see page 61). Discuss the rest of the assignment.

7. Have students fill out the "Loan Payment Chart" to determine how many years it will take to pay off the car loan. Students may need more than one chart if they chose a very expensive car.

8. Guide students in making bar graphs to show relationships between interest, principal, and time.

9. Ask students to present their graphs to other students to demonstrate what they've learned about the relationship between interest and principal.

Extension Ideas

Talk about the other expenses involved in car ownership. Students can investigate insurance, parking, and gas costs as well. Discuss the other expenses young people first living on their own would have. Record these expenses, and then figure out how much income this lifestyle would require.

Notes

Name _____ Date _____

BUYING THE CAR OF MY DREAMS
Assignment Sheet

You've just started a great new job, but you need a car to get there. A relative has offered to lend you money to help you buy a new car—the car of your dreams! Here's the arrangement:

- Your relative will charge you the lowest interest rate for car loans that you can find, based on current interest rates from lenders in your community.

- After studying your finances, you've determined that you can spend $6,000 a year on your car loan.

- You will put a regular monthly payment into a savings account each month and then make one $6,000 payment to your relative every 12 months.

- You may continue making annual payments until the car is paid for, no matter how long it takes.

This project helps you see what it costs to buy a car. Real-world auto financing is a bit more complex, but understanding the costs of borrowing money is the first step in making sound financial decisions.

For this project, you will research how much your car costs and what interest rate you will pay, and then calculate how long it will take you to pay off your loan.

When you borrow money, there are two important terms to understand: *principal* and *interest*. When you ask a bank or credit union for a loan, you ask for the amount that you need to make the purchase. This is called the *principal*. Banks and credit unions, however, don't lend money for free. They make money by charging people for the money they lend. *Interest* is the money they charge you for borrowing. The interest you pay is calculated as a percentage of what you owe. The simplest interest is calculated using an *annual percentage rate* (APR). For example, if you borrow $1,000 at a 10% APR, you will owe $1,100 at the end of one year. Here's how to figure this out:

$$\text{\textbf{P x R x T = I}}$$
Principal x Rate of interest x Time = Interest owed

$$\$1,000 \times \frac{10\%}{\text{year}} \times 1 \text{ year} = \$100$$

$1,000 (Principal) **x 10% per year** (Rate) **x 1 year** (Time) **= $100** (Interest)

The total amount you owe on the loan at the end of the first year is principal plus interest:

P + I = total owed
$1,000 + $100 = $1,100

Challenging Projects for Creative Minds © 1999 by Phil Schlemmer and Dori Schlemmer. Free Spirit Publishing Inc.
Minneapolis, MN 1-800-735-7323 <www.freespirit.com>. This page may be reproduced for home or classroom use.

57

Name _____ Date _____

BUYING THE CAR OF MY DREAMS
Researching Principal and Interest

1. Decide what kind of new car you want to buy and find out how much it costs. You can look at many places to figure out how much the car of your dreams will cost. You can call or visit a car dealership, compare auto prices on the Internet, or check in newspapers or reference books. Ask a parent for help if you need to.

  Be sure to include sales tax and other charges for your car. Document where you got your information.

CAR DATA	WHERE DID YOU GET YOUR DATA?
Make, model, and color: _____	_____
_____	_____
Base Price: $ _____	_____
Extras:	_____
_____ + $ _____	_____
_____ + $ _____	_____
_____ + $ _____	_____
Total Car Price = $ _____	_____
Sales Tax + $ _____	_____
License plates + $ _____	_____
Other Charges + $ _____	_____
Principal = _____	_____

2. What's the best car loan interest rate you can find? You may be able to find bank and credit union interest rates in the local newspaper, or you can call lenders and ask for their lowest new car loan interest rates. You can also check sites on the Internet. Check at least three sources because interest rates can vary.

LENDER	ANNUAL RATE	WHERE DID YOU GET YOUR DATA?
1.		
2.		
3.		

Best Interest Rate _____ %

3. Calculate the interest for the first year of your car loan. (Use a calculator.)

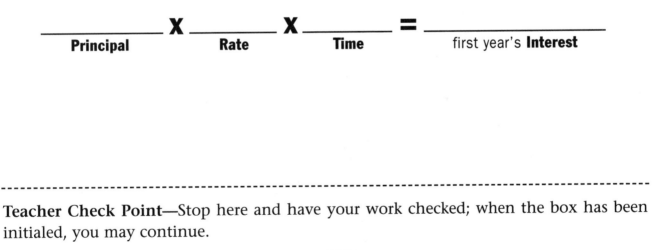

_____ X _____ X _____ = _____
  Principal   **Rate**   **Time**   first year's **Interest**

- -

Teacher Check Point—Stop here and have your work checked; when the box has been initialed, you may continue.

OK to Continue

Challenging Projects for Creative Minds © 1999 by Phil Schlemmer and Dori Schlemmer. Free Spirit Publishing Inc. Minneapolis, MN 1-800-735-7323 <www.freespirit.com>. This page may be reproduced for home or classroom use.

BUYING THE CAR OF MY DREAMS
Figuring the First Year's Costs

Complete the chart below for the first year of your loan.

Principal:	
Annual interest rate:	
Total annual payment:	$6,000
Amount of annual payment that is interest:	
Amount of annual payment that is principal:	
Total amount put into savings each month:	
Amount of monthly savings that is interest:	
Amount of monthly savings that is principal:	
New principal after annual payment:	

- -

Teacher Check Point—Stop here and have your work checked; when the box has been initialed, you may continue.

OK to Continue

BUYING THE CAR OF MY DREAMS

Loan Payment Chart

Fill out a column on the chart below for each year until you completely repay your loan. Be sure to use the data from the "Figuring the First Year's Costs" chart in the first column. Turn the completed chart in for a Teacher Check Point.

Principal: ....

Annual interest rate: ....

Total annual payment: ....

Amount of annual payment that is interest: ....

Amount of annual payment that is principal: ....

Total amount put into savings each month: ....

Amount of monthly savings that is interest: ....

Amount of monthly savings that is principal: ....

New principal after annual payment: ....

YEAR: ___	YEAR: ___	YEAR: ___	YEAR: ___	YEAR: ___	YEAR: ___

How much will you eventually pay for the car? $ _____

Teacher Check Point—Stop here and have your work checked; when the box has been initialed, you may continue.

OK to Continue ☐

Challenging Projects for Creative Minds © 1999 by Phil Schlemmer and Dori Schlemmer. Free Spirit Publishing Inc.

BUYING THE CAR OF MY DREAMS

Principal and Interest Bar Graph

Make a bar graph to show the relationship between annual interest payments and annual principal payments each year. Make one bar for each year of data; use two colors. Be prepared to present your graph and explain what it shows.

What color will the bars for principal (P) be? _____

What color will the bars for interest (I) be? _____

	YEAR 1	YEAR 2	YEAR 3	YEAR 4	YEAR 5	YEAR 6	YEAR 7	YEAR 8	YEAR 9	YEAR 10
$ 6,000										
$ 5,000										
$ 4,000										
$ 3,000										
$ 2,000										
$ 1,000										
$ 0										

Challenging Projects for Creative Minds © 1999 by Phil Schlemmer and Dori Schlemmer. Free Spirit Publishing Inc.

Buying the Car of My Dreams: Standards of Quality

TASK	QUALITY STANDARD
1. Select a dream car for the project and research the costs.	Correctly record the make, model, and color of the new car.
2. Calculate the principal for a car loan.	Calculate the loan principal by accurately adding the car's sticker price, sales tax, license fees, and additional charges.
3. Research the rate of interest for the loan.	Contact three local lenders and record the lowest new car loan interest rate from each, and then select the lowest of the three rates to use for the project.
4. Use the formula P x R x T = I.	Accurately calculate the amount of interest due at the end of each year of the loan, based on the principal and the annual interest rate.
5. Complete a chart of the first year of the loan.	Accurately calculate monthly savings required and the remaining interest and principal due after the first year.
6. Complete the "Yearly Loan Payment Chart."	Accurately calculate and record the principal and interest data for each year of the loan.
7. Determine how many years it will take to pay off the loan.	Accurately fill out the "Loan Payment Chart" until the "new principal" is zero or less than zero.
8. Produce a graph to show annual interest payments and annual principal payments.	Develop a two-color bar graph that is carefully constructed, properly labeled, and accurate. The graph shows the relationship between principal and interest over the entire life of the loan.
9. Explain what the graph shows about principal, interest, and time.	Demonstrate understanding of the relationships and trends illustrated on the graph by presenting it orally and answering questions about it.

Name _____ Date _____

How Did I Do?

SELF   **TEACHER**

I Used These Skills:

I followed directions carefully and fully. ....

I identified a "dream car" for my project. ....

I conducted research to find information about the price of the car. ....

I conducted research to find information about local interest rates. ....

I applied math skills to correctly calculate the principal for my loan. ....

I used the formula P x R x T = I to correctly calculate interest. ....

I applied math skills to correctly complete the "Loan Payment Chart." ....

I used my knowledge of graphs to plot data from the chart. ....

I explained my graph orally and answered reasonable questions. ....

I finished tasks on time. ....

I Made These Things:

I completed the "Researching Principal and Interest" handout. ....

I completed the "Figuring the First Year's Costs" handout. ....

I completed the "Yearly Loan Payment Chart." ....

I produced a two-color bar graph (annual interest and principal). ....

I Learned These Things:

I know how to use the formula P x R x T = I. ....

I understand the role interest plays in repaying a loan. ....

I discovered the relationship between interest and principal over time. ....

I understand how to use graphs to illustrate loan repayments. ....

I figured out how long it would take to pay off a car loan. ....

I can explain how this project worked and answer questions about it. ....

I know how to use a calculator for percentage problems. ....

Comments: _____

_____

_____

_____

_____

PART 3

People & Places

Home Sweet Home

Beginning Level

To young children, home and family are the center of their world. In their families, children learn they are loved and belong, and they develop their values and self-concept. This project helps students think about the diversity of families. They will get an opportunity to think about their own families and describe the things that make home and family special to them, and each student will contribute to a classroom exhibit. Students will likely be able to see that there are many different kinds of families—large and small, two-parent and single-parent, blended families and extended families—and that students have a variety of places that they call home, whether it's an apartment or a house or some other kind of home.

During the project students will:

1. Draw family portraits.

2. Make maps of their bedrooms or other special rooms in their homes.

3. Tell why their homes are sweet.

4. Display their work in the classroom.

MATERIALS

- poster board or art paper (optional)
- pencils and crayons or markers

STUDENT HANDOUTS

- Family Portrait
- My Special Place
- My Home Is Sweet
- How Did I Do?

CONCEPTS

- *family*—the people you are related to or share a special close relationship with
- *special place*—a place that makes you feel good
- *portraits*—pictures of people
- *mapping*—showing locations through visual means

Note: Talking about family and home can be difficult for some children for a variety of reasons. Some children live with foster parents or in temporary shelters, and it's possible that some children may feel ashamed of their families or where they are living. In cases like these, use your knowledge of the child's situation as well as your own discretion and make adaptations to the assignment as needed.

Project Steps

1. Introduce the project to the students. Tell them they will create an exhibit for the classroom called "Home Sweet Home," and they will explore the ideas of family and home. They will look at the many different kinds of families and the places that are special to students in the class. Students will think about the question "What makes home so sweet?" by looking at some of the things people love about home: the special people, special places, and other special things. Introduce the "Standards of Quality" (see page 72) so students know what you expect of them.

2. Hand out the "Family Portrait" form (see page 69). Tell students to draw the people who live in their homes for the exhibit. Ask that they draw everyone who lives in their home, including themselves, and pets if they'd like. They can also include other family members who visit frequently and help make their home a special place. Explain that they should use their best efforts and that they should write the names of each person in the portrait next to that person. Describe what they can do to make their drawings look good for the final exhibit:

- Draw each person in pencil first.
- Write the name of each person in the picture (you may need to help them).
- Use crayon or markers to color hair, clothes, pets, and other details.
- Sign their finished portraits.

3. Explain that students will draw a detailed picture or a map that shows their favorite place in their homes. Model the process by drawing a picture of the classroom on the chalkboard. Ask students to guide you in drawing an "overhead" view of the room, as if they were in a helicopter looking down, through the roof, at the classroom. Ask questions to get them started:

- What shape is the room?
- Where is the door?
- Where are the windows?
- Where should we draw the teacher's desk?
- How can we show the student desks?
- What else should we show?

Talk about your finished drawing, and show them how it relates to the classroom.

4. Give students the "My Special Place" handout to take home (see page 70). Tell them that for the museum exhibit, they will draw a special place in their homes, just as they drew the classroom. They can pick their favorite room to draw—their bedroom, the room where the family gathers in the evenings, the kitchen, or any place they feel is special to them. Remind them that the drawing of their special room should show its shape, the location of doors and windows, and one or two pieces of furniture. Encourage students to get help at home for this assignment. Ask students to explain why this is a special room. (Young students may dictate their explanations.)

5. Give students the "My Home Is Sweet" handout (see page 71). Remind them that they've drawn portraits of their families and mapped out their special place. Explain that now it's time to think of other things that make home a "sweet" place to live. Older students can write and draw their responses, while younger ones can make drawings or dictate responses.

6. Ask each student to present his or her work to the rest of the class before adding it the "Home Sweet Home" museum exhibit in the classroom. As students talk, make a master list of what students say helps make their home sweet. Ask students to think about the differences and similarities between families and homes and encourage them to talk about the differences in positive ways. Point out the strong points in the work that they've done and how each piece contributes to the whole of the exhibit. Just as each student belongs to a family, they each belong and are an important part of the class.

Extension Ideas

Provide materials so students can create a cover for their finished drawings and writing and gather them into a book. Their "published" family album could include a title, drawings of their homes, their names as writer and illustrator, and decorative elements.

Notes

_____

_____

_____

_____

_____

_____

_____

_____

_____

_____

_____

Name _____ Date _____

HOME SWEET HOME
Family Portrait

Who lives in your home? Draw everyone who lives in your home (pets too!). Write everyone's name on the drawing.

In my home you will find:

Name _____ Date _____

HOME SWEET HOME
My Special Place

What room or other place in your home is special to you? Draw your special place. Ask someone at home to help you. Show these things:

1. the shape of the room
2. the doors and windows
3. some furniture
4. other details that might show why this room is special

What place did you choose? _____

I like this place because _____

_____

_____

Challenging Projects for Creative Minds © 1999 by Phil Schlemmer and Dori Schlemmer. Free Spirit Publishing Inc.
Minneapolis, MN 1-800-735-7323 <www.freespirit.com>. This page may be reproduced for home or classroom use.

Name _____ Date _____

HOME SWEET HOME
My Home Is Sweet

Why is your home a sweet place to live? Give two reasons.

My home is sweet because _____

_____

_____

_____

My home is sweet because _____

_____

_____

_____

Home Sweet Home: Standards of Quality

TASK	QUALITY STANDARD
1. Draw a family portrait.	Draw a portrait of the people (and pets) who live in their home. The portrait is well organized and properly labeled, and it represents their best art skills.
2. Draw a picture titled "My Special Place."	Draw a special place. The place is properly identified, and the drawing is carefully constructed and well organized, showing the shape of the room, the location of doors and windows, and at least one or two pieces of furniture. The drawing also includes a clear explanation of why this is the student's special place.
3. Explain why home is "sweet."	Describe in words or with drawings at least two reasons why home is a sweet place. Written descriptions are clear and use proper vocabulary. Picture descriptions are well organized, easily recognized, and represent good art skills. (Students with limited writing skills may dictate their descriptions.)

Name _____ Date _____

HOME SWEET HOME
How Did I Do?

Put a ✓ after each goal that was met.

	STUDENT	TEACHER
	☺	☺

I Used These Skills:
I followed directions. . . . .
I used my best art skills. . . . .
I used my best writing skills. . . . .

I Made These Things:
I drew a picture of the people I live with. . . . .
I told who the people in my home are. . . . .
I drew a picture of my special place. . . . .
I told why the place is special. . . . .
I told why my home is sweet. . . . .
I helped make a classroom exhibit. . . . .

I Learned These Things:
I know what it means to be a family. . . . .
I know how to draw a picture of a room. . . . .
I know how to write about my home. . . . .
I thought about why my home is sweet. . . . .
I know that families are alike in some ways. . . . .
I know that families are different in some ways. . . . .

Comments: _____

_____

_____

_____

_____

_____

Challenging Projects for Creative Minds © 1999 by Phil Schlemmer and Dori Schlemmer. Free Spirit Publishing Inc. Minneapolis, MN 1-800-735-7323 <*www.freespirit.com*>. This page may be reproduced for home or classroom use.

American Heroes

Intermediate Level

One way to make history more meaningful is to learn about people who have made important contributions to our world. Who are some of these people? Why did they become well known? What effect did they have on the world?

In this project, students work in pairs (or small groups) to research an American hero and nominate that person to be honored on a postage stamp. Students will highlight their hero's accomplishments and background and explain why their hero deserves such recognition.

During the project students will:

1. Work in a team of two or three students to explain a hero's accomplishments.

2. Make a sign for the display.

3. Develop a set of "Did You Know?" sheets.

4. Produce a poster-sized stamp of the hero.

5. Explain in their own words why this person is a hero.

6. Create a slogan, poem, or cartoon about their hero.

7. Present their hero's best qualities.

- reference materials for researching famous Americans

- poster board, paper, paints, markers, scissors, and/or other art supplies (for making posters)

- postage stamps to show as examples (optional)

- Assignment Sheet

- Did You Know?

- In My Own Words

- How Did I Do?

- *hero*—someone with admirable qualities

- *research*—locating and using relevant information

Project Steps

1. Before presenting the project to students, develop a list of American heroes suitable for students to research. Be sure the list is ethnically diverse and includes both men and women. You may use the list below as a guide toward developing your own list to fit your school's curriculum or the resources that you have available. This project works very well in conjunction with a thematic unit on topics such as explorers or writers or political figures.

Martin Luther King, Jr. Florence Nightingale
Jim Thorpe Frederick Douglass

Amelia Earhart   Walt Disney
Jackie Robinson   Albert Einstein
Cesar Chavez   Ralph Waldo Emerson
Abraham Lincoln   Rosa Parks
Susan B. Anthony   Benjamin Franklin
Black Elk   Helen Keller
Harriet Tubman   Satchel Paige
George Washington   Eleanor Roosevelt
Thomas Jefferson   Geronimo
Malcolm X   Emily Dickinson

Decide in advance how students will choose partners and what parameters to give students in choosing the heroes they will study. It's important to give students some choice in deciding who to research, but you want variety in their subjects. (Note: If your class intends to submit their ideas to the U.S. Postal Service for consideration, keep in mind that the people stamps portray cannot be living.)

2. Introduce the project to students. Tell them they will be learning about people that many consider heroes. Talk with your students about the concept of a *hero*. What does it mean to be a hero? Who are their heroes? Why are heroes important? What can we learn from the examples others have set? Students will explore these issues in this project.

Talk about the scenario for the project: The U.S. Postal Service is about to begin work on a new series of stamps recognizing American heroes. Students will work together to study the lives of well-known Americans and prepare displays that show why these people should be honored with a commemorative stamp. Students will present their finished displays and explain their reasons for including the hero in the new postage stamp series.

3. Divide the students into pairs (or small groups) and distribute all three project handouts. Tell students that they will:

- Choose a hero to nominate.

- Make a sign that gives relevant facts about the hero.

- Create a large poster of their stamp that illustrates one of their hero's accomplishments.

- Record two interesting facts about the hero on the "Did You Know?" form (see page 78).

- Write essays on why their hero deserves to be honored.

- Create one more item for the display, such as a slogan, a pennant, a poem.

- Post their displays to share with other students.

Discuss the requirements of the project and the "Standards of Quality" (see page 80), and answer any questions.

4. Because students must conduct research for the project, discuss how they can start gathering information for their displays and guide them to appropriate resources. You may want to model the process for students with a very well-known American (for example, Abraham Lincoln), showing where you find your information, asking the class to help put it into context, and creating a sample display.

5. Allow students time to complete their research, and make yourself available to answer questions and help throughout the process.

6. Make bulletin board space available to display the finished work. You may spread the display down your hallway, over several bulletin boards or walls in your classroom, or even on a single bulletin board, displaying each postage stamp exhibit for two or three days. Ask each group to present their work to the rest of the class and to explain why their hero deserves to be honored with a stamp.

7. Ask students to reflect on what they've learned through the process, not only about the accomplishments of the heroes they studied, but also about what it takes to be considered a hero.

Hold a class discussion or ask students to reflect on the project in writing. Has their definition of a hero changed or become clearer during the process? Can they see anything they've done in their own lives that might be considered heroic? Perhaps they stood up to a bully, volunteered at a food pantry, or helped others in an emergency.

Help students see that the little things they do every day are as important as the big accomplishments and that the small steps and goals we fulfill mark progress on the way to fulfilling bigger dreams.

Extension Idea

Submit your students' stamp ideas to the United States Postal Service and perhaps they might inspire a stamp or series of stamps. For information:

United States Postal Service
The Citizens' Stamp Advisory Committee
c/o Stamp Management
U.S. Postal Service
475 L'Enfant Plaza, SW, Room 4474EB
Washington, DC 20260-6756
http://www.usps.gov

The Web site has the U.S. Postal Service's guidelines for stamp subject selection, as well as lists of stamp subjects for the past five years. Subject selections should be submitted at least three years in advance of the proposed date of issue to allow enough time for consideration and for design and production if the subject is approved. Here's a summary of the criteria the Post Office uses for selecting stamps of famous Americans (you can write for complete guidelines):

1. No living person will be honored on a stamp.

2. Stamps honoring individuals will usually be issued in conjunction with significant anniversaries of their birth, but no sooner than ten years after that person's death. (U.S. presidents are the only exception.)

3. Only subjects with national appeal will be considered.

4. Stamps shall not be issued to honor individuals whose principal achievements are associated with religious undertakings or beliefs.

5. No subject will be considered for a stamp if it has already appeared within the past ten years.

Name _____ Date _____

AMERICAN HEROES
Assignment Sheet

The U.S. Postal Service is looking for well-known American heroes to honor on a postage stamp—and you get an opportunity to nominate someone. You'll work with a partner to choose a hero, research his or her accomplishments, and make a display showing others why your hero deserves to be honored with a postage stamp.

Answer the first two questions, then read the assignment carefully to find out what you will do to complete the project.

1. Who is your partner? _____

2. Who is the hero you will study? _____

3. Work together to make a sign about your hero. Write your hero's name in big letters and include the hero's:

- birth date (day, month, and year)
- date of death
- hometown and state (if your hero moved around a lot, do the best you can to tell where he or she came from)
- accomplishments (what your hero is known for)

4. Work together to design a large poster of a postage stamp commemorating your hero. Include a portrait or drawing showing something about your hero. For example, if your hero is teacher and astronaut Christa McAuliffe, you could draw her in her space suit or draw the space shuttle taking off. Include a caption on your poster to explain what it shows. Remember, your goal is to show why this person is a great American hero.

5. Each partner will record two interesting facts about the hero on the "Did You Know?" form. These forms are for display, so remember to make them neat and well written.

6. Each partner will write about the hero's accomplishments using the handout "In My Own Words." Try to answer these questions: Why do you consider this person a hero? What did this person do that made a difference in the world? Again, these are for display and should be neat and well written.

7. Work with your partner to create one more item for your display:

- Write a slogan for your hero. (A slogan is a short, catchy saying that will help people remember your hero. For example, "Thomas Edison Had a Bright Idea.")
- Draw a cartoon about your hero.
- Write a poem about your hero.
- Design a pennant touting your hero. For example, you could write "Jackie Robinson: First African-American Major League Baseball Player" and illustrate it.

8. Work together with your partner to tell the class about your hero. Explain why this person deserves to be honored on a postage stamp.

Did You Know?

American Hero:

Did you know that _____

_____

_____

_____

_____

_____

Did you know that _____

_____

_____

_____

_____

_____

Written by: _____

In My Own Words

— American Hero: —

Why is this person a hero? _____

_____

_____

_____

_____

_____

_____

_____

_____

_____

_____

_____

Written by: _____

American Heroes: Standards of Quality

TASK	QUALITY STANDARD
1. Work cooperatively with a partner.	Offer thoughtful input, contribute to the final display, accept others' ideas, show sufficient effort, and remain on task.
2. Choose a topic.	Willingly pursue an appropriate topic.
3. Conduct research.	Apply research skills to locate information on the hero they are studying.
4. Produce a sign for the bulletin board.	Contribute to making a sign that meets all the assignment requirements. The sign is carefully laid out and contains accurate information with all words correctly spelled.
5. Create a large poster of your stamp for the bulletin board.	Contribute to a poster that meets all assignment requirements. The poster is carefully laid out in the form of a postage stamp, visually appealing, and factually correct with all words correctly spelled.
6. Complete the handout "Did You Know?"	Identify two interesting facts about the hero and record them on the "Did You Know?" handout using their best writing skills. Each partner chooses different facts to record.
7. Complete the handout "In My Own Words."	Explain why the person is a hero, using original arguments written in their own words and using their best writing skills.
8. Produce an additional item for the display.	Contribute to making one of these items: slogan, cartoon, poem, or pennant. The item is carefully laid out and demonstrates creative thinking.

Name _____ Date _____

AMERICAN HEROES
How Did I Do?

	STUDENT			TEACHER		
	I DID BETTER THAN I EXPECTED	I DID AS WELL AS I EXPECTED	I NEED MORE TIME	STUDENT DID BETTER THAN I EXPECTED	STUDENT MET MY EXPECTATIONS	STUDENT NEEDS MORE TIME

I Used These Skills:

I followed directions.						
I found information about the hero.						
I used my best art skills.						
I used my best writing skills.						
I wrote information on my handouts.						
I helped to design a quality sign.						
I helped to design a quality poster.						
I worked well with others.						
I finished tasks on time.						

I Made These Things:

I helped make a sign about the hero.						
I helped make a poster about the hero.						
I finished two handouts:						
• Did You Know?						
• In My Own Words.						
I helped make one more display item.						
I helped design the bulletin board.						

I Learned These Things:

I studied an American hero.						
I know when my hero was born.						
I know where my hero was born.						
I know when my hero died.						
I know where my hero died.						
I know why my hero is famous.						
I know interesting facts about my hero.						
I can tell why the person is a hero.						

Comments: _____

Trading Card Hall of Fame

Advanced Level

In this project, students learn about important topics in social studies by designing trading cards. Working as designers for Cards of Knowledge, Inc., each student will produce a large mock-up of a trading card for the company's new Hall of Fame series. The cards they create will serve as educational resources in the classroom, offering well-researched information on a person, place, or event that has had an impact on world history.

During the project students will:

1. Choose a historic person, place, or event.

2. Conduct research to find out more about their topic.

3. Create a large, fully developed mock-up of a trading card following a set of standard requirements.

4. Present their cards to an audience, showing how their cards fit the requirements.

5. Display the card in a "Hall of Fame" exhibit.

MATERIALS

- reference materials for research on categories you identify
- poster board (11" x 17" or larger)
- art supplies for creating colorful trading card mock-up posters
- Topic Selection Class Record

STUDENT HANDOUTS

- Assignment Sheet
- Trading Card Requirements Checklist
- How Did I Do?

CONCEPTS

- *research*—locating and using relevant information
- *cause*—something that brings about a certain result or effect
- *effect*—something that inevitably follows an event or cause
- *time line*—a graphic showing important events in order within a specific time period
- *references*—sources of information that you use for research
- *standards*—an established set of requirements that something is judged against.

Project Steps

1. Before you begin, decide what topics you'd like students to explore in this project. You can choose an area that meets requirements in your school's curriculum. For example, if you are studying world geography, you could have students research the significance of world monuments such as the Eiffel Tower, the Statue of Liberty, and the Great Wall of China. Individualize the project to fit your goals for your students.

2. Decide how to let students choose their topics. There are several ways you can approach topic selection to make sure each student has a unique topic and you have enough resources to go around:

- **Free choice.** You can let students choose any social studies topic that interests them, and assign topics on a first-come, first-served basis.

- **Teacher list.** You can create your own list of topics and let students choose from that list.

- **Class list.** You can let the class brainstorm its own list of possible topics focused on the material you've covered in class.

- **Textbook list.** You can let students choose any topic they find mentioned in their social studies textbook. Some teachers direct students to choose topics from sections of the textbook they do not plan to cover in the regular curriculum. This lets students develop greater breadth of learning.

Resource availability is an important factor in this project. Talk with your school media specialist or librarian, and preview available resource materials to make sure students can find enough information about the topics they choose.

3. Give students the "Assignment Sheet" (page 85) and discuss each step of the project. Talk about the "Standards of Quality" (see page 87) so students understand what's expected of them. Distribute the "Trading Card Requirements Checklist" (see page 86) and read through it with students. This handout describes all the components that each card must have to be included in the Hall of Fame.

4. Provide time for students to reflect on possible topic choices. You may want to let them explore several topics before they settle on one. Approve their choices, and record their topics on the "Topic Selection Class Record (see page 88)."

5. Conduct the project, allowing ample time for research, planning, poster development, and oral presentations. Guide students along the way. If you ask students to make first draft copies of their trading cards, be sure to allocate enough time.

6. Ask each student to present his or her completed trading card to the rest of the designers. They should focus on showing how their card meets the requirements of the project and talk about some of the decisions they made in making their card.

7. Designate a space for a Trading Card Hall of Fame on a wall in your classroom or school, and display the completed work.

Extension Idea

Ask students to create smaller versions of their trading cards on index cards or on a multimedia software program such as HyperStudio. Students can combine their cards to make a set of trading cards.

Notes

_____

_____

_____

_____

_____

_____

_____

_____

_____

_____

_____

_____

_____

Name _____ Date _____

TRADING CARD HALL OF FAME
Assignment Sheet

You're a designer at Cards of Knowledge, Inc., a company that publishes educational trading cards for use in schools. The company plans to introduce a new set of cards on important people, places, and events in world history. You want to work on this new Hall of Fame trading card series. Your job is to develop a prototype of one card for the series. You'll present your poster-sized model to a group of fellow designers to show that it meets all the requirements necessary to become a part of the set.

1. Choose a topic and record it on the line below. Your supervising editor from Cards of Knowledge, Inc., will provide guidelines on choosing a topic for the Hall of Fame series. You'll be responsible for researching your topic for information to include on your final card.

Topic: _____

☐ Editor's OK

☐ Please see the editor about your topic.

2. Examine the "Trading Card Requirements Checklist." These are the standards for the trading cards. If you can demonstrate that your card has all the necessary parts, done at a high level of quality, and if you present your project effectively, it will be included in the Hall of Fame trading card series.

3. Develop a plan for your trading card. What information do you know? What information do you need? You may want to make a first draft of the card to make sure your plan makes sense, looks good, and works in the space that you have available.

4. Create a large model of your trading card. Remember, in the publishing world, as in any business, quality matters. Be neat, accurate, and thorough.

5. Present your trading card model to an audience of fellow designers, all of whom worked on the same project and were responsible for the same requirements. Show them how your card meets the standards on the "Trading Card Requirements Checklist." Talk about your project and why your card should be included in the Hall of Fame trading card series.

Name _____ Date _____

TRADING CARD HALL OF FAME
Trading Card Requirements Checklist

Designers will present trading cards that include the following:

☐ A clear topic that fits the supervising editor's guidelines.

☐ A carefully drawn border.

☐ A well organized card design that is easy to follow and understand.

☐ At least one picture with an informative caption.

☐ A written explanation about why this topic is significant.

☐ An accurate time line showing six events related to the topic.

☐ A description of an early event that caused your topic to become important.

☐ A description of a later event that your topic affected.

☐ A "Did You Know?" or "Factoid" section that includes relevant facts.

☐ A list of three references where people could find more information on the topic.

Designers will effectively present their cards to the other designers. When presenting, they will point out the relevant features of their cards and do the following:

☐ Speak clearly and slowly enough for everyone to hear.

☐ Speak expressively.

☐ Make eye contact with audience members.

☐ Demonstrate understanding of the topic.

☐ Answer audience questions about the topic.

☐ Listen respectfully when others are talking.

Trading Card Hall of Fame: Standards of Quality

TASK	QUALITY STANDARD
1. Identify a topic that fits the editor's guidelines.	Follow class guidelines to choose an appropriate topic, one with enough information available to complete the project requirements.
2. Develop a time line that includes the topic.	Use research skills to discover at least six events to include on a time line about your topic. The time line correctly shows events leading up to the topic and related events that follow. Each event is correctly placed and briefly described.
3. Create a picture that illustrates the topic.	Create a graphic or illustration that is carefully drawn and shows something interesting, unusual, or thought-provoking about the topic. It includes a caption that helps explain why the topic is important.
4. Write about why the topic is important.	Write a brief essay that explains the historical significance of the topic and encourages the reader to learn more about it.
5. Describe an event that caused the topic to happen or become important.	Note an event on the time line that helped cause the topic to occur or become historically important, and explain the cause and effect relationship between the event and the topic. The reader should understand that the topic was significantly affected by an event that happened before it on the time line.
6. Describe an effect of the topic.	Note an event on the time line that was affected or caused by the trading card topic. Explain the cause and effect relationship between the topic and the event. The reader should understand that this event was significantly affected by the topic.
7. Collect facts for a "Did You Know?" or "Factoid" section on the trading card.	Gather interesting, relevant facts that will help a reader understand the topic. The facts will be loosely connected but stand on their own without extensive explanation so that they can be read in any order without losing meaning.
8. List three references where people could learn more about the topic.	Record complete and accurate references for at least three sources of information on the topic. Sources students used for this project should be cited.
9. Create a model trading card about the topic that includes all of the above information.	Design and produce a large model of the trading card. The card is carefully laid out, with attention to appearance and ease of use. All of the required elements are included.
10. Present the trading card to the class.	Present their trading cards to their classmates, explaining how they have met all of the project requirements in their final trading cards.

Name_____ Date _____

TRADING CARD HALL OF FAME
Topic Selection Class Record

STUDENT NAME	APPROVED TOPIC

Name_____ Date _____

TRADING CARD HALL OF FAME

How Did I Do?

SELF TEACHER

I Used These Skills:

I followed directions carefully and fully. ....

I identified a topic that fits the requirements. ....

I conducted research to find information about my topic. ....

I used my best writing skills. ....

I analyzed events to identify cause and effect relationships. ....

I used my best art skills to design a card. ....

I presented my work orally and showed that I met all the requirements. ....

I finished tasks on time. ....

I Made These Things:

I created a time line of events. ....

I created an illustration. ....

I wrote an essay on why my topic is important. ....

I explained the causes and effects of my topic. ....

I developed a "Did You Know?" section for the trading card. ....

I made a list of at least three resources about my topic. ....

I created a large model of the trading card. ....

I Learned These Things:

I learned how and where to find information about my topic. ....

I identified important reasons for learning about my topic. ....

I learned about cause and effect relationships. ....

I learned how to make a time line. ....

I discovered interesting facts about my topic. ....

I gained experience making oral presentations. ....

Comments: _____

_____

_____

_____

_____

PART 4

Research

Did You Know?

Beginning Level

This project helps you introduce students to the concept of research, looking for answers to questions. In this project, students assume the role of "Did You Know?" experts. They form a team of researchers who produce educational collages that schools can use to introduce a wide variety of topics and interesting information.

This project can be easily adapted to fit into your existing curriculum. You may want to have students focus their research and findings on a particular theme such as animals or maps or the environment. Or you may simply ask students to look for facts that interest them. However you decide to set this up, be sure to have a wide variety of resources available in your classroom or resource center.

During the project students will:

1. Choose topics that interest them.

2. Produce "Did You Know?" cards for the collage.

3. Display the finished collage in the classroom or elsewhere in the school.

MATERIALS

- large roll of paper
- reference books, magazines, and other resources
- paste or tape
- art materials: colored paper, markers, crayons, yarn, other decorative pieces

STUDENT HANDOUTS

- Did You Know? cards (words)
- Did You Know? cards (words and pictures)
- Did You Know? cards (pictures)
- How Did I Do?

CONCEPTS

- *fact*—a true piece of information
- *research*—to look for information (Research can be done using many different sources: books, magazines, newspapers, Web sites, surveys, interviews.)
- *experts*—people who have a lot of knowledge in one area
- *collage*—a collection of pictures and words arranged artistically and attached to a flat surface

Project Steps

1. Cut a piece of roll paper large enough to fill an available wall space in the classroom or elsewhere in the school. Write "Did You Know?" in large letters across the top edge of the paper.

2. Introduce students to the project. Talk to students about facts and research to make sure they understand the concepts. Many people start research by asking two questions: What do I know already? and What do I want to know? Model for students how you might use these questions in locating interesting facts in the resources you have available. Decide how many cards each student should make for the class collage. Let students know how many cards they will make.

3. Hand out the "Did You Know?" card forms. Notice that there are three different styles: words (page 95), words and pictures (page 96), and pictures (page 97). You may decide which is most appropriate for your students, let them ask for the forms they prefer, or require that they use a combination of styles. Model filling these out for your students. Talk about the "Standards of Quality" (see page 98) to clarify the expectations for the project.

4. Provide time and resources for students to identify interesting facts to show or tell on their cards. Create a resource center in your classroom, or arrange for time in the media center so media specialists can help students as needed. Make sure each student has the proper number of cards, and have extras on hand in case of mistakes.

5. Students should work carefully to record their facts on their cards. Be available to answer questions as students are working.

6. When the cards are finished, collect them and check for quality, using the guidelines you explained to the students. Each card has a place for the teacher to check when it is ready to be attached to the collage.

7. Ask students to tell the rest of the class what they have written or drawn on their cards. This will let them demonstrate what they know even if their writing or drawing skills are limited.

8. After each student presents his or her information, he or she can paste or tape the cards to the collage.

9. Display the finished collage on a wall in the room or elsewhere in the school.

Extension Idea

Let students make placemat collages to bring home. Supply poster board for students to attach their favorite facts and drawings to form a collage. Laminate the placemats.

Notes

_____
_____
_____
_____
_____
_____
_____
_____
_____
_____
_____
_____
_____
_____
_____
_____
_____
_____
_____
_____

Did You Know?

_____

_____

_____

_____

_____

_____

_____

By:_____ Teacher OK ☐

Did You Know?

_____

_____

_____

_____

_____

_____

_____

By:_____ Teacher OK ☐

Did You Know?

_____
_____
_____
_____
_____
_____
_____

By:_____ Teacher OK ☐

Did You Know?

_____
_____
_____
_____
_____
_____
_____

By:_____ Teacher OK ☐

Did You Know?

By:_____ Teacher OK ☐

Did You Know?

By:_____ Teacher OK ☐

Did You Know?: Standards of Quality

TASK	QUALITY STANDARD
1. Choose topics to research.	Use reference materials to identify interesting, appropriate topics to include on the "Did You Know?" collage. (Each card may be about a different topic.)
2. Record facts on cards.	Record one interesting fact on each card (either in writing, through drawing, or in a combination of the two).
3. Explain what each card says, shows, or means.	Explain clearly what each card says, shows, or means.
4. Produce the required number of information cards.	Create the minimum number of cards required.
5. Apply writing skills.	Demonstrate their best writing skills on each card with written words.
6. Apply art skills.	Demonstrate their best art skills on each card with pictures.
7. Attach each card to the "Did You Know?" collage.	Carefully attach each information card onto the collage.

Name _____ Date _____

DID YOU KNOW?
How Did I Do?

Put a ✓ after each goal that was met.

	STUDENT	TEACHER
	☺	☺

I Used These Skills:
I followed directions. . . . .

I found facts in books or other sources. . . . .

I used my best writing skills. . . . .

I used my best art skills. . . . .

I wrote information correctly. . . . .

I told the class about my "Did You Know?" cards. . . . .

I Made These Things:
I made "Did You Know?" cards. . . . .

I worked on a "Did You Know?" collage. . . . .

I Learned These Things:
I know what research is. . . . .

I made "Did You Know?" cards about:

● _____ . . . .

● _____ . . . .

● _____ . . . .

● _____ . . . .

● _____ . . . .

Comments: _____

_____

_____

_____

_____

_____

Alien Encyclopedia

Intermediate Level

This project can provide a fun introduction to research and encyclopedias. Students act as scientists who have received a message from a civilization on a distant planet requesting information about life on Earth. The scientists have decided to put together an encyclopedia on topics that aliens from another planet would find interesting. As a class, they develop a list of topics and conduct research before writing reports for the book that will be sent.

During the project students will:

1. Choose a topic for their article.

2. Conduct research to find information about the topic.

3. Write an article that describes and explains the topic.

4. Produce at least one illustration to accompany the article.

5. Give the article a simple title that clearly identifies the topic.

6. Insert the article alphabetically into the *Alien Encyclopedia*.

MATERIALS

- reference materials (media center or library)
- large three-ring binder
- alphabetical divider tabs for the binder
- three-hole punch
- art supplies (for illustrations)

STUDENT HANDOUTS

- Assignment Sheet
- Encyclopedia Article
- Encyclopedia Illustration
- How Did I Do?

CONCEPTS

- *encyclopedia*—a book that has articles on many topics. General encyclopedias come in many volumes and contain information on almost every topic you can imagine. Special encyclopedias focus on one broad topic area, such as science, music, or writers.

- *research*—finding specific information to answer a question

- *copyright*—protects authors' ownership of their writing and pictures. No one else has the right to copy them. Just as authors and illustrators own their writing and pictures, student's have copyright in theirs. Copyright dates tell when a piece was written and can usually be found in the front of a book following the symbol ©.

CONCEPTS continued. . .

- *facts*—true, verifiable information

- *notetaking*—recording facts from other sources by writing down key words and phrases

Project Steps

1. Set up the *Alien Encyclopedia* in a large three-ring binder with alphabetical divider tabs.

2. This project is designed to get kids thinking about their lives. It asks, How would we represent ourselves and our world to people who know nothing at all about our planet? It gives kids an opportunity to let others see the world through their eyes. You can use this project to tie in to a specific curriculum area you are studying (maybe the aliens have a particular interest in plant or animal life, weather, or world government). Or you can give your students free reign to choose any topic that interests them and that they want to share with the aliens. Sometimes it's easier for children to select topics if you give them guidelines.

3. The project is also designed to help kids think about doing research, taking notes, and writing a short, factual article based on that information. If you emphasize this part of the project, you may want to go to the media center so students can examine encyclopedias before they write their articles. Let students look at the books and then hold a discussion. Ask students to talk about how encyclopedias are organized, what kind of information they include, and how illustrations help them understand the information.

4. Introduce the project to the students. Tell them that as scientists, they will do research to create articles for an alien encyclopedia. They will need to find at least three sources of information on their topic, take notes from their resources, and create articles with illustrations. Be sure to preteach any skills your students may be unfamiliar with.

5. Give students the three project handouts. Go through the assignment steps and the "Standards of Quality" (see page 107).

6. Remind the students that your role is editor-in-chief. You'll approve all their work on the encyclopedia from their topic choice to their article and illustration. You'll help them locate resources, and guide them through the process of taking notes and drafting their articles. You'll also review their work before they write their final drafts on the handout.

7. When their final drafts are finished and you've approved them, students can insert them into the encyclopedia binder in alphabetical order. Either you or the students can punch holes in their final articles so they fit neatly into the binder. (Note: If you create an expanding *Alien Encyclopedia* that continues year after year, it's worth the effort to put reinforcement rings on the pages or have the pages laminated, so that they can be removed and handled without harm.)

Extension Ideas

Use desktop publishing to put your *Alien Encyclopedia* on a disk. Students can key their articles into a document and scan their illustrations to publish a professional-looking encyclopedia. Each student can bring a copy home.

Notes

Name _____ Date _____

ALIEN ENCYCLOPEDIA
Assignment Sheet

You are a scientist who has received a message from outer space. Aliens on a distant planet want information about life on Earth. You and your fellow scientists will put together an encyclopedia to send them. Your job is to write and illustrate an article for the encyclopedia. Here's your assignment.

1. Choose a topic for your encyclopedia article. The topic is your choice, but it must be approved by the editor-in-chief. Record the topic you want to write about on the line below; then turn in the assignment sheet to get approval.

Topic: _____

☐ Editor's OK

☐ Please see the editor about your topic.

2. Begin researching your topic. You need to be well informed about the topic before you can write an article about it. Ask yourself what you already know and what you need to find out. Locate at least three resources with information on your topic. List them below:

TITLE	AUTHOR	PUBLISHER	COPYRIGHT DATE
1.			
2.			
3.			

3. Your editor has asked you to take notes while you study. Write down the most important and interesting facts that you find from each source. Don't copy exactly what's in your source. Put your notes in your own words. It helps if you write down key ideas and phrases rather than complete sentences. You'll combine the information in your notes to write your article.

4. You need at least one picture to go along with your article. Decide what you will draw to illustrate your article. Take notes for your picture, too. Make a quick sketch in pencil to show what you want to include. This will be your first draft of your picture.

5. Write a first draft of the article. Use your own words so that it sounds like you wrote it. Do you have all the information you need to explain your topic? If not, go back and do more research. Your article should be one page long. You will need permission to make it longer. Remember to include an introduction paragraph, supporting details, and a conclusion.

6. Turn in the first draft of the article. The editor will set up a meeting with you to discuss your work. Prepare for your meeting by thinking about your article. Listen to your editor's suggestions and revise your article.

7. Write the final draft of your article on an "Encyclopedia Article" handout.

8. Turn in your draft drawing. The editor will set up a meeting with you to discuss your work and talk about ways to improve it.

9. Make the changes that you and the editor agree need to be made. Add color to finish the drawing and then erase unwanted pencil lines and marks.

10. Put the article and illustration into the *Alien Encyclopedia* in the correct place alphabetically.

Encyclopedia Article

Title:_____

_____

_____

_____

_____

_____

_____

_____

_____

_____

_____

_____

_____

_____

_____

_____

_____

Author:_____ Copyright Date:_____

Encyclopedia Illustration

Title:_____

Caption: _____

_____

Author:_____ Copyright Date: _____

Alien Encyclopedia: Standards of Quality

TASK	QUALITY STANDARD
1. Choose a topic for an article.	Choose a topic that is appropriate for the grade level and readily researched.
2. Conduct research.	Apply research skills by finding at least three sources of information about the topic and identifying important and interesting facts to include in the article.
3. Take good notes from sources.	Write notes in their own words.
4. Write a first draft article.	Write a one-page article using information discovered through research. Articles are written in the students' own words, not copied from research materials.
5. Meet with the "editor" about the first draft.	Meet with the teacher to discuss possible revisions, accept constructive advice, and offer ideas for improving the article.
6. Produce a final draft article.	Write a final one-page article on the handout, based on the conference with the editor/teacher. Final articles show the student's best writing skills and demonstrate understanding of the topic.
7. Create a "pencil draft" illustration.	Create an illustration to supplement the article. The draft is done in pencil.
8. Meet with the "editor" about the proposed illustration.	Meet with the editor/teacher to discuss the illustration, accept constructive advice, and offer recommendations for improving the illustration.
9. Produce a finished illustration.	Revise the illustration if necessary and add color, erasing all unwanted pencil marks. The illustration provides additional information or shows some aspect of the topic graphically and represents their best art skills.
10. Insert the article in the *Alien Encyclopedia*.	The student correctly inserts a finished article and illustration into the encyclopedia.

Name_____ Date _____

ALIEN ENCYCLOPEDIA
How Did I Do?

	STUDENT			TEACHER		
	I DID BETTER THAN I EXPECTED	I DID AS WELL AS I EXPECTED	I NEED MORE TIME	STUDENT DID BETTER THAN I EXPECTED	STUDENT MET MY EXPECTATIONS	STUDENT NEEDS MORE TIME

I Used These Skills:

I followed directions.						
I used my best writing skills.						
I used my best art skills.						
I used research skills to find information.						
I took notes in my own words.						
I combined facts into an article.						
I designed an illustration.						
I improved my first draft using feedback from others.						
I finished tasks on time.						
I filed my article alphabetically.						

I Made These Things:

I wrote a first draft article.						
I wrote an improved final draft article.						
I drew a "pencil draft" illustration.						
I drew an improved final illustration.						

I Learned These Things:

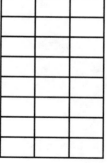
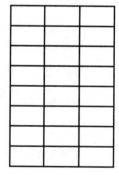

I know how encyclopedias work. ....

I studied this topic for an article: _____

_____ ....

I found interesting facts for the article. ....

I know more about the topic now. ....

I learned about editing. ....

I learned how to improve my writing. ....

I learned how to illustrate an article. ....

Comments: _____

_____

_____

_____

Software Design Company

Advanced Level

While older elementary students have usually developed an understanding of how books work and may feel comfortable creating their own, they may not have begun to think about creating CD-ROM or Web-based documents. In this project, students become "software developers" who produce educational CD-ROMs. While they don't actually produce the CDs, they create a plan that shows how computer users will navigate through the program. Students will choose a topic to research, design pictures and text for four screens, and show how to navigate among the screens. Students create a prototype on paper to illustrate how the CD would look if it were produced.

For this project, students don't need to work on a computer, nor do you need a computer in your room. It can be helpful, however, to demonstrate CD-ROMs to students so they clearly understand what they're being asked to do.

During the project students will:

1. Learn about the design of CD-ROM or Web-based documents.

2. Research a topic of personal interest.

3. Create an outline of information for their computer program.

4. Plan and lay out at least four linked computer screens about their topic.

5. Display and explain their finished work.

MATERIALS

- reference books for research
- drawing materials for creating "screen" graphics and web diagrams

STUDENT HANDOUTS

- Assignment Sheet
- CD Information Plan Sheet
- Computer Screen template (four copies per student)
- Hot Buttons
- Web Control
- Project Sample (to use as a model for the project)
- How Did I Do?

CONCEPTS

- *CD-ROM*—a computer disk that stores sound, image, and text information
- *home page*—the first page or screen on a CD-ROM or Web site. It introduces you to what you'll find elsewhere on the CD or at the site.
- *buttons and links*—highlighted images or text that you click on to go from one place to another
- *outline*—a way of organizing information into topics and subtopics
- *web diagrams*—a way of organizing information in a nonlinear fashion

Project Steps

1. Introduce the project to the students, previewing what they know about CD-ROMs and how they present information. Introduce the concept of using web diagrams—organizing or presenting information in a nonlinear manner. Information on Internet sites and CD-ROMs is organized into webs. Viewers move through the text by clicking on buttons when they want more information on a specific topic. If you have a computer in the room, demonstrate how this works using a CD-ROM or your school's Web site. Before they proceed with the project, students must have a solid understanding of the nonlinear webbing inherent in this type of computer programming.

2. Distribute the "Assignment Sheet" (see page 112) to the students and discuss the project step by step. Talk about the Standards of Quality (see page 125).

3. Give students the "CD Information Plan Sheet" (see page 114). Each student will choose a topic (for example, bottlenose dolphins) and record it on the planning sheet. Approve their topics before they begin their research.

4. Make sure students understand how to take notes and how to create an outline, and then provide ample time for research. Have students identify three subtopics and record them on their plan sheets (for example, bottlenose dolphin adaptations, echolocation, and catching food).

5. Guide students in completing their plan outline. They will record at least three facts for each subtopic, plus three general facts. Remind them to record the facts in their own words rather than copying directly from their sources. The plan they create will serve as an outline for the computer program they are developing and will help you discuss how an outline is different from an information web. Even though the information looks linear on the plan sheet, students will later see how it can be webbed.

6. After students have gathered their notes into a plan outline, they will decide how to link the information on their CD-ROMs. Students will create buttons and links on the computer screens they invent and show where you "go" when you click on each one.

7. Give each student four blank "Computer Screen" handouts (see page 115). Students will use the forms to illustrate what their screens will look like and to record the specific information that viewers will learn when they "click" the buttons. Go through the handouts with the students before they begin. (A complete sample project is provided to illustrate what these worksheets might look like.)

- Point out that each screen template has a button named "Go Home" in the lower right corner. Explain that viewers should never have to travel through a computer program without having a simple way to get home. The "Go Home" button is the return route to the first screen (home page).

- Point out that each screen template has three additional buttons along the bottom edge of the screen. These buttons are named "Facts," "Action," and "Go to." Students will add a more detailed subtitle for each button on their screens. For example, "Facts: Dolphin Adaptations," or "Action: Dolphins at Play (movie)," or "Go to: Echolocation."

8. Give students the "Hot Buttons" worksheet (see page 116). Explain that this handout will guide them in defining what happens when each button is clicked. (See sample on page 123.)

9. Give students the "Web Control" handout (see page 117). Explain that they will show graphically how all of the screens are linked. They will draw lines between the buttons and the screens to which they are linked. (The sample project on page 124 illustrates what this worksheet might look like.)

10. Provide space on a wall or bulletin board to display student work, or allow students to present their projects orally.

Extension Ideas

- Offer students the option of expanding their projects beyond four screens. Allow this option only after the student completes the original four at or above the expected level of quality. For increased complexity, students can draw new buttons and link their work with other students' projects.

- If you have the equipment and the knowledge—or if you can find a volunteer who can help—encourage kids to develop their programs into a Web site or a simple multimedia program.

- Encourage students to present their facts in a more lively presentation, such as a computer game or within a story. Let them look at CD-ROM games for ideas on how to do this.

Notes

_____

_____

_____

_____

Name _____ Date _____

SOFTWARE DESIGN COMPANY
Assignment Sheet

You are a software developer who creates CD-ROMs for schools. You've been asked to design a new CD-ROM that the company hopes to sell next year. Your teacher will serve as your product development director on this project. Follow the assignment below to complete your job.

1. Choose a topic that interests you and that you think other students would be interested in learning about. Remember, you are planning an educational software product. You may choose to create a program about a person, a place, an animal, a topic in your favorite subject at school, or an activity you enjoy. Try to choose something you're familiar with but have questions about. Get approval for your topic before you begin.

Topic: _____

☐ Director's OK

☐ Please see the director about your topic.

2. All of the information you include in your CD-ROM design must be accurate. You'll need to do research to answer questions that you have and to find facts about your topic. Locate at least three resources that can help you find the information you need. List them below:

TITLE	AUTHOR	PUBLISHER	COPYRIGHT DATE
1.			
2.			
3.			

3. You'll receive a "CD Information Plan Sheet" from your director. You'll use this handout to create an outline for your CD-ROM. Record your approved topic at the top. Then record three subtopics related to your main topic. For example, if your topic is bottlenose dolphins, you might choose to find out more information on adaptations, echolocation, and catching food. Finally, conduct research to learn more about your topic. List three general facts about your main topic, plus three detailed facts for each subtopic. (See the example.)

4. Use the "Computer Screen" handout to design four screens that users will see when they navigate through your CD.

5. Think of a title for your CD-ROM and record it on each worksheet.

6. Name each screen. Call the screen that users see when they start the program "Home." Title the rest of the screens to fit the three subtopics you identified on the "CD Information Plan Sheet." (For example, the screens for the bottlenose dolphin CD are named "Home," "Echolocation," "Adaptations," and "Catching Food."

7. Design the Home screen on your first "Computer Screen" worksheet. What do you want others to see when the program opens? This screen is like the topic sentence in a paragraph: it introduces the subject and gives clues to what else is there. Your Home screen will include links to your three subtopics and tie everything together. (You can cover up the "Go Home" button on your Home screen since you're already there.)

8. It's time to work with buttons. Buttons are special spots highlighted on the screen that users can click to make something happen. Notice that there are four buttons at the bottom of each screen. You will decide what happens when each is clicked:

Facts: Give this button a complete name. For example, "Facts: Bottlenose Dolphins." Refer to your "CD Information Plan Sheet," and record at least three general facts that users will learn when they click the "Facts" button. These facts will pop up onto the screen when viewers click on the "Facts" button.

Action: Give this button a complete name. For example, "Action: Dolphins Playing." Action buttons link to sounds or movement. They can play video or audio clips, run animation, pop-up graphs or illustrations, and so forth. What actions would people be interested in for your topic?

Go to: Give this button a complete name. "Go to" buttons link users to another screen. For example, "Go to: Echolocation" takes users to a screen that tells about how dolphins use echolocation to find objects in the water.

The **Go Home** button in the lower right corner allows the user to return to the Home screen at any time.

9. Develop the remaining three screens. Record your facts from your "CD Information Plan Sheet." Be creative in your presentation. Include additional facts on the screen itself or develop a theme that visually links the screens.

10. Use the "Hot Buttons" handout to explain what happens when a user clicks the buttons you have invented. Record the screen name, tell what you named each button, and describe what happens when each button is clicked.

11. Use a "Web Control" worksheet to show how a user can navigate between the four screens by clicking "Go to" buttons.

12. Present your CD-ROM design by displaying it on a bulletin board or wall. Be prepared to explain your work and to answer questions from your teacher and classmates.

113

Name _____ Date _____

SOFTWARE DESIGN COMPANY
CD Information Plan Sheet

Main Topic for CD: _____

General Information

Fact: _____

Fact: _____

Fact: _____

Subtopic 1: _____

Fact: _____

Fact: _____

Fact: _____

Subtopic 2: _____

Fact: _____

Fact: _____

Fact: _____

Subtopic 3: _____

Fact: _____

Fact: _____

Fact: _____

Name _____ Date _____

SOFTWARE DESIGN COMPANY
Computer Screen

CD-ROM Title: _____

Screen Name: _____

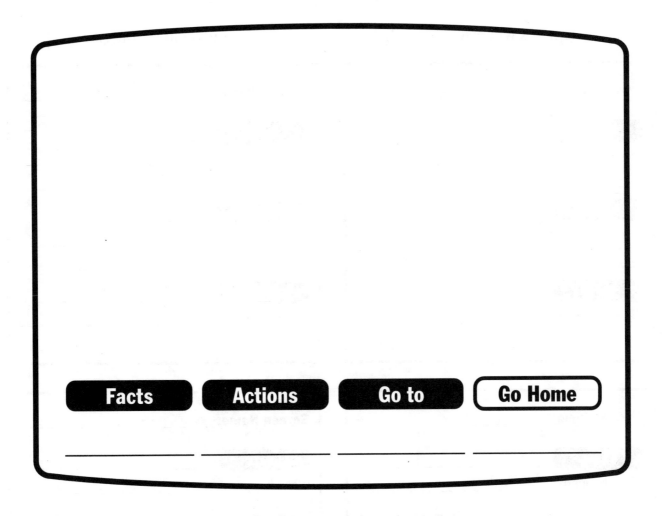

Facts	Actions	Go to	Go Home

Record three facts that users will learn by clicking the "Facts" button:

1. _____

2. _____

3. _____

Developed by: _____ Copyright Date: _____

Name_____ Date_____

SOFTWARE DESIGN COMPANY

Hot Buttons

CD-ROM Title: _____

Software Developer:_____

Tell what happens when someone clicks each button in your CD-ROM program.

Screen Name: _____

Facts _____
What happens? _____
_____

Actions _____
What happens? _____
_____

Go to _____
What happens? _____
_____

Screen Name: _____

Facts _____
What happens? _____
_____

Actions _____
What happens? _____
_____

Go to _____
What happens? _____
_____

Screen Name: _____

Facts _____
What happens? _____
_____

Actions _____
What happens? _____
_____

Go to _____
What happens? _____
_____

Screen Name: _____

Facts _____
What happens? _____
_____

Actions _____
What happens? _____
_____

Go to _____
What happens? _____
_____

Name _____ Date _____

SOFTWARE DESIGN COMPANY
Web Control

CD-ROM Title: _____

Software Developer: _____

Use colored arrows to show how your screens are linked so users can navigate between them. The rectangles below are small models of the computer screens you have designed. Record the names of the screens, then draw an arrow from each button to the screen it's linked to. (Some buttons aren't linked to other screens, so don't draw arrows from them.)

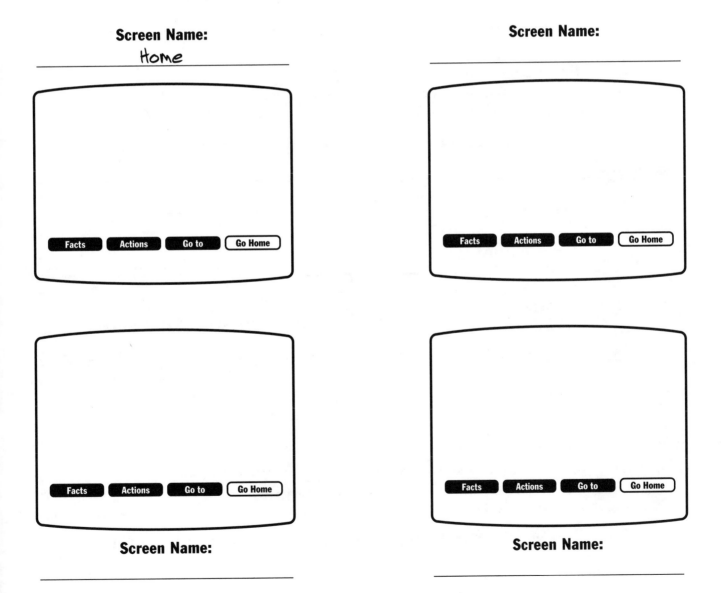

Screen Name:
Home

Facts   Actions   Go to   Go Home

Screen Name:
_____

Facts   Actions   Go to   Go Home

Facts   Actions   Go to   Go Home

Screen Name:
_____

Facts   Actions   Go to   Go Home

Screen Name:
_____

Name _____ Date _____

SOFTWARE DESIGN COMPANY
CD Information Plan Sheet (sample)

Main Topic for CD: Bottlenose Dolphins

General Information

Fact: There are 25 species of saltwater dolphins.

Fact: Dolphins enjoy playing in the water. They are fun-loving animals.

Fact: Dolphins are mammals. They are warm-blooded, give live birth, and breathe with lungs.

Subtopic 1: Echolocation

Fact: Dolphins locate objects underwater by making clicking sounds. These clicks bounce off of objects and back through the dolphin's lower jaw to the inner ear.

Fact: The clicks start in the nasal cavity, then go through a part of the forehead called the "melon."

Fact: Dolphins can send up to 2,000 clicks per second.

Subtopic 2: Adaptations

Fact: Dolphins are torpedo shaped so that water flows over them easily.

Fact: Dolphins have a dorsal fin that helps keep them straight in the water when they swim.

Fact: Dolphins have a clear jelly-like substance in their eyes to protect them from salt in the water.

Subtopic 3: Catching Food

Fact: Dolphins eat almost any sea animal, but their favorite foods are fish and squid.

Fact: Dolphins have very sharp teeth for grabbing and holding fish, but they don't chew their food. They swallow fish whole, head first.

Fact: Dolphins often hunt as a team, herding fish into a tight group and then taking turns feeding.

Challenging Projects for Creative Minds © 1999 by Phil Schlemmer and Dori Schlemmer. Free Spirit Publishing Inc.
Minneapolis, MN 1-800-735-7323 <www.freespirit.com>. This page may be reproduced for home or classroom use.

Name_____ Date_____

SOFTWARE DESIGN COMPANY
Computer Screen (sample)

CD-ROM Title: Bottlenose Dolphins_____

Screen Name: Home_____

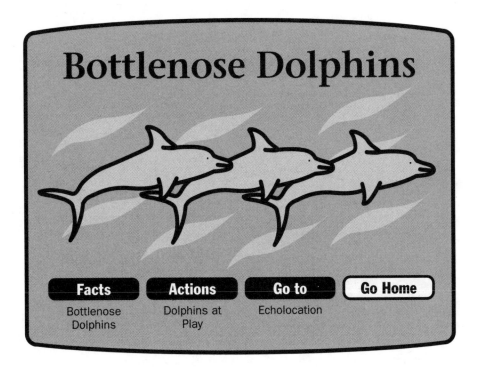

Record three facts that users will learn by clicking the "Facts" button:

1. There are 25 species of saltwater dolphins._____

_____

2. Dolphins enjoy playing in the water. They are fun-loving animals._____

_____

3. Dolphins are mammals. They are warm-blooded, give live birth, and

breathe with lungs._____

Developed by: Erin Schlemmer_____ Copyright Date: 1999_____

Name _____ Date _____

SOFTWARE DESIGN COMPANY
Computer Screen (sample)

CD-ROM Title: Bottlenose Dolphins

Screen Name: Echolocation

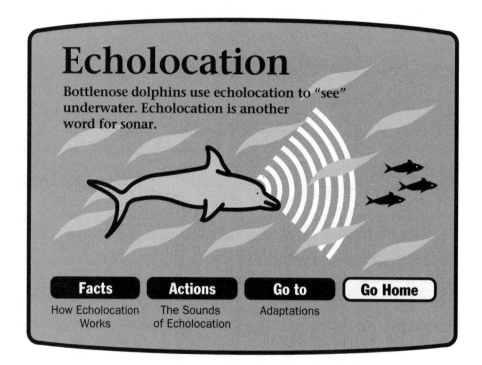

Record three facts that users will learn by clicking the "Facts" button:

1. Dolphins make clicking sounds that bounce off of objects and back through the dolphin's lower jaw to the inner ear.

2. The clicks start in the nasal cavity, then go through a part of the forehead called the "melon."

3. Dolphins can send up to 2000 clicks per second.

Developed by: Erin Schlemmer   Copyright Date: 1999

Name _____ Date _____

SOFTWARE DESIGN COMPANY
Computer Screen (sample)

CD-ROM Title: Bottlenose Dolphins _____

Screen Name: Adaptations _____

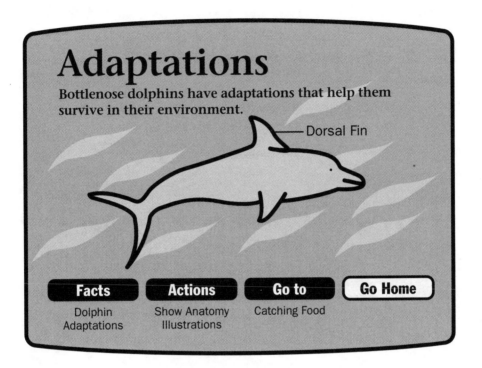

Record three facts that users will learn by clicking the "Facts" button:

1. Dolphins are torpedo shaped so that water flows over them easily.

2. Dolphins have a dorsal fin that helps keep them straight in the water when they swim.

3. Dolphins have a clear jelly-like substance in their eyes to protect them from salt in the water.

Developed by: Erin Schlemmer _____ Copyright Date: 1999 _____

Name _____ Date _____

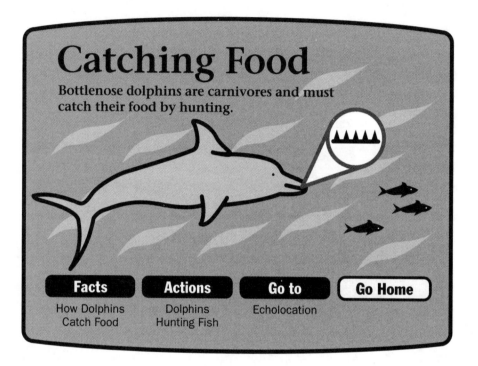

SOFTWARE DESIGN COMPANY
Computer Screen (sample)

CD-ROM Title: Bottlenose Dolphins

Screen Name: Catching Food

Catching Food
Bottlenose dolphins are carnivores and must catch their food by hunting.

Facts	Actions	Go to	Go Home
How Dolphins Catch Food	Dolphins Hunting Fish	Echolocation	

Record three facts that users will learn by clicking the "Facts" button:

1. Dolphins eat almost any sea animal, but their favorite foods are fish and squid.

2. Dolphins have very sharp teeth for grabbing and holding fish, but they don't chew their food. They swallow fish whole, head first.

3. Dolphins often hunt as a team, herding fish into a tight group and then taking turns feeding.

Developed by: Erin Schlemmer   Copyright Date: 1999

Name _____ Date _____

SOFTWARE DESIGN COMPANY

Hot Buttons (sample)

CD-ROM Title: _Bottlenose Dolphins_

Software Developer: _Erin Schlemmer_

Tell what happens when someone clicks each button in your CD-ROM program.

Screen Name: _Home_

Facts	_Bottlenose Dolphins_

What happens? _Shows facts about bottlenose dolphins._

Actions	_Dolphins at Play_

What happens? _Runs a movie of dolphins playing in the ocean._

Go to	_Echolocation_

What happens? _Takes you to a screen that tells how dolphins use echolocation._

Screen Name: _Echolocation_

Facts	_How Echolocation Works_

What happens? _Shows facts about how dolphins use echolocation._

Actions	_The Sounds of Echolocation_

What happens? _Plays a sound clip of the clicking noise dolphins make to create "echoes."_

Go to	_Adaptation_

What happens? _Takes you to a screen that tells all about dolphin adaptations._

Screen Name: _Adaptations_

Facts	_Dolphin Adaptations_

What happens? _Shows facts that describe and explain dolphin adaptations._

Actions	_Show Anatomy Illustrations_

What happens? _Pops up a series of illustrations that show how a dolphin's body is built._

Go to	_Catching Food_

What happens? _Takes you to a screen that tells what dolphins eat and explains how they catch food._

Screen Name: _Catching Food_

Facts	_How Dolphins Catch Food_

What happens? _Shows facts about dolphin diet, hunting methods, and eating habits._

Actions	_Dolphins Hunting Fish_

What happens? _Runs an animation that shows different ways that dolphins chase and catch fish._

Go to	_Echolocation_

What happens? _Takes you to a screen that tells how dolphins use echolocation to catch food._

Name _____ Date _____

SOFTWARE DESIGN COMPANY

Web Control (sample)

CD-ROM Title: **Bottlenose Dolphins**

Software Developer: **Erin Schlemmer**

Use colored arrows to show how your screens are linked so users can navigate between them. The rectangles below are small models of the computer screens you have designed. Record the names of the screens, then draw an arrow from each button to the screen it's linked to. (Some buttons aren't linked to other screens, so don't draw arrows from them.)

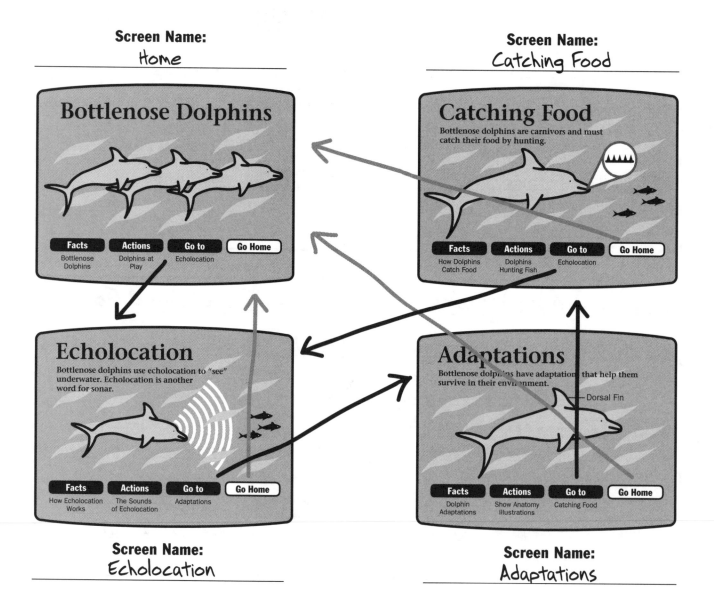

Screen Name:
Home

Screen Name:
Catching Food

Screen Name:
Echolocation

Screen Name:
Adaptations

Software Design Company: Standards of Quality

TASK	QUALITY STANDARD
1. Choose a topic and identify subtopics for the project.	Identify a topic and three subtopics appropriate for an educational software product.
2. Conduct research and complete a "CD Information Plan Sheet."	Record the main topic for the CD and three related subtopics on the plan sheet; find and record three general facts about the main topic and three interesting facts for each subtopic (twelve facts in all).
3. Think of a title for the CD-ROM product.	Provide a clear title for the CD-ROM.
4. Design four computer screens.	Use their best creative thinking and graphic art skills to design four screens on "Computer Screen" worksheets. All screens have identifying titles. Each worksheet includes three clearly written facts linked to the "Facts" button.
5. Create three buttons on each of the screens.	Determine the function for each button. Buttons have titles, and they link to other parts of the program, show facts, or initiate an action on the current screen.
6. Define the function of each button.	Identify each button on the Hot Buttons worksheet and define its function by clearly and concisely describing what happens when a user clicks it.
7. Describe how a user can navigate within the program.	Create a web diagram using arrows to indicate the links between "Go to" buttons and screens.
8. Present the CD-ROM design.	Display the completed "Computer Screens," "Hot Buttons," and "Web Control" handouts, and explain the work and answer reasonable questions about it.

Name _____ Date _____

SOFTWARE DESIGN COMPANY
How Did I Do?

SELF   TEACHER

I Used These Skills:

I followed directions carefully and fully. ....

I identified an acceptable topic for an educational software product. ....

I identified at least three subtopics for my CD-ROM screens. ....

I conducted research to find accurate information for my project. ....

I applied creative thinking skills to design four computer screens. ....

I applied my best graphic art skills to produce final computer screens. ....

I applied organization/systems skills to develop 12 interactive buttons. ....

I used my best writing skills. ....

I finished tasks on time. ....

I Made These Things:

I completed a "CD Information Plan Sheet." ....

I designed and created four computer screens. ....

I recorded three accurate, related facts on each screen worksheet. ....

I gave three buttons on each screen a complete name. ....

I described what each button does on a "Hot Buttons" worksheet. ....

I designed a "Web Control" worksheet to show how screens are linked. ....

I created a display to show my finished work. ....

I Learned These Things:

I discovered at least twelve interesting facts about my topic. ....

I learned what "buttons" on a computer screen do. ....

I learned about the different functions a computer button can have. ....

I learned about linking screens in a computer program to make a web. ....

I learned how to make a web diagram showing graphically how information is related. ....

I understood my project well enough to explain it to others. ....

I answered questions about my project. ....

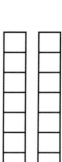

Comments: _____

_____

_____

PART 5

Resources

Name _____ Date _____

 # Choosing a Topic

Deciding on a topic can be the hardest part of beginning a project. Let's say you want to do a project on dogs. That's a good start, but you need to think about that topic and do some research before you can narrow that down to a size that's easy to work with. Do you want to study only one breed of dog? What do you want to find out about dogs? Breeds? Dog training? Working dogs? Choose something you find fun and interesting.

Use this form as you begin your research to help you narrow your topic. Start by thinking and browsing through a book or library. You may find

the perfect topic right away. Or you might need time to talk to other people or check to see that you can find enough information about your topic. Here's one way to start:

1. What general category are you interested in?

2. What are some specific topics in that category?

3. Begin your research to find out more specific subtopics for each topic above.

4. Look over your subtopics and choose one, or look for a theme that could be the focus of your project.

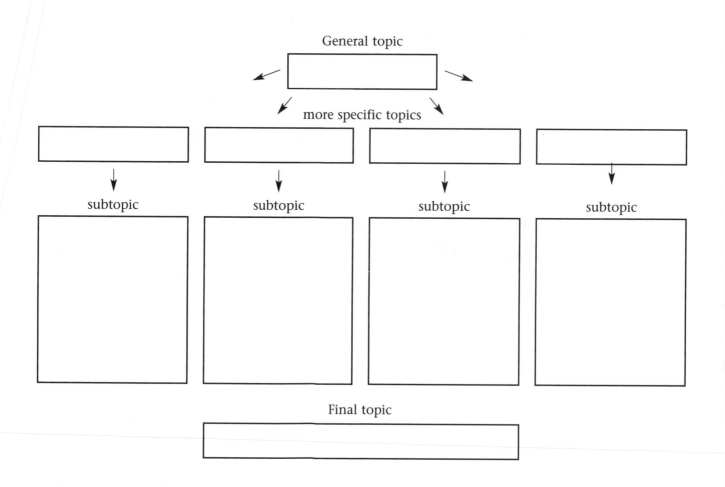

Name _____ Date _____

Finding Resources

Project title: _____ Project Due Date: _____

Getting Started

Briefly describe the topic of your project. What are you going to study?

_____

_____

_____

Finding Information

What information do you need?

_____

_____

_____

_____

_____

What resources can you use to find information? (Think about all the places you might look for information: people, libraries, the Internet, CD-ROMs, newspapers, businesses, government offices, historical societies, videos.) List possible resources below:

1. _____

2. _____

3. _____

4. _____

5. _____

Name _____ Date _____

 # Taking Notes

When you do research, you usually find more information than you can remember. That's why you should take notes. Notes help you remember facts and remind you where you found your information. Some people take notes on index cards. Other people take notes in a special notebook. Or you can use the form on this page. No matter what you write on, one good way to take notes is to make an outline.

   Outlines help you organize the information that you find. To make an outline, you can identify the main ideas that you want to remember and the details that support that main idea. For example, if you were taking notes for an essay on Benjamin Franklin:

Benjamin Franklin—inventor
- proved lightning and electricity were the same force
- invented bifocal glasses
- designed the Franklin stove

   Always take notes in your own words—don't copy exactly. Remember that research means finding information from many sources and putting it together in your own special way. If you do copy exact words from a source, or quote from an interview, you must use quotation marks and let your readers know whose words you are borrowing.

   Use this worksheet to make your own outline notes of the resources you'll use for your project.

Title of source: _____

Author: _____ Date of publication: _____ Page numbers: _____

1. Main idea: _____
- Detail: _____
- Detail: _____
- Detail: _____

2. Main idea: _____
- Detail: _____
- Detail: _____
- Detail: _____

3. Main idea: _____
- Detail: _____
- Detail: _____
- Detail: _____

Challenging Projects for Creative Minds © 1999 by Phil Schlemmer and Dori Schlemmer. Free Spirit Publishing Inc. Minneapolis, MN 1-800-735-7323 <*www.freespirit.com*>. This page may be reproduced for home or classroom use.

Name _____ Date _____

Planning Your Writing

Title _____

Introduction _____

_____

Main idea #1 _____

Supporting details

1. _____

2. _____

3. _____

Main idea #2 _____

Supporting details

1. _____

2. _____

3. _____

Main idea #3 _____

Supporting details

1. _____

2. _____

3. _____

Conclusion _____

_____

_____

Name _____ Date _____

 # A-OK Editing Checklist for Beginning Authors

Title _____

MOK (Meaning OK?)

☐ Does it make sense?

☐ Are my facts correct?

☐ Did I say what I wanted to?

SOK (Sentence OK?)

☐ Does it express a complete thought?

☐ Does it start with a capital letter?

☐ Does it end with the correct punctuation mark?

WOK (Word OK?)

☐ Is it the very best word?

☐ Is it spelled correctly?

☐ Is it capitalized correctly?

NOK (Neatness OK?)

☐ Is it easy to read?

☐ Does it follow the format required by my teacher?

Name _____ Date _____

A-OK Editing Checklist

Title _____

MOK (Meaning OK?)

☐ Does it make sense?

☐ Is it concise and to the point?

☐ Is it complete?

☐ Are my facts correct?

☐ Did I say what I really wanted to say?

☐ Is there an introduction?

☐ Is there a conclusion?

POK (Paragraph OK?)

☐ Is it indented?

☐ Is it made up of sentences related to one main idea?

☐ Is it connected logically with paragraphs that come before or after?

SOK (Sentence OK?)

☐ Does it express a complete thought?

☐ Does it start with a capital letter?

☐ Does it end with the correct punctuation mark?

☐ Do the subject and verb agree?

WOK (Word OK?)

☐ Is it the very best word?

☐ Is it spelled correctly?

☐ Is it capitalized correctly?

NOK (Neatness OK?)

☐ Is it easy to read?

☐ Does it follow the format required by my teacher?

Further Reading

Bibliography

Armstrong, Thomas. *Multiple Intelligences in the Classroom.* Alexandria, VA: ASCD, 1994.

Branscomb, H. Eric. *Casting Your Net: A Student's Guide to Research on the Internet.* Needham Heights, MA: Allyn & Bacon, 1997.

Gardner, Howard. *Frames of Mind: The Theory of Multiple Intelligences.* New York: Basic Books, 1993.

Jensen, Eric. *Introduction to Brain-Compatible Learning.* San Diego, CA: The Brain Store, 1998.

Schlemmer, Phil. "A Learning-to-Learn Curriculum Model." *Changing Schools* (October 1995): 8–9.

———. "Curriculum Development: Quality Education in a Budget-Cutting Age." *Illinois School Research and Development.* (Fall 1981): 22–86.

———. *Learning on Your Own.* New York: The Center for Applied Research in Education, 1987. (A five-volume series.)

Schumm, Jeanne Shay, and Marguerite Radencich. *School Power: Strategies for Succeeding in School.* Minneapolis: Free Spirit Publishing, 1992.

Smutny, Joan Franklin; Sally Yahnke Walker, and Elizabeth A. Meckstroth. *Teaching Young Gifted Children in the Regular Classroom.* Minneapolis: Free Spirit Publishing, 1997.

Winebrenner, Susan. *Teaching Kids with Learning Difficulties in the Regular Classroom.* Minneapolis: Free Spirit Publishing, 1996.

Books for Students

How to be School Smart: A Super Study Guide by Elizabeth James, Carol James, and Carol Barkin (New York: Beech Tree Books, 1998). Filled with helpful strategies and practical hints, this resource covers all aspects of schoolwork—from notetaking to handling homework. Ages 9–12.

Kingfisher First Animal Encyclopedia by John Farndon and Jon Kirkwood. (New York: Kingfisher, 1998). Surveys animals from aardvark to zebra, including information on diet, habits, and environment. Ages 5–8.

National Geographic World Atlas for Young Explorers (Washington, DC: National Geographic, 1998). In addition to maps, this volume offers information on map reading, endangered species, photographs, and more. Ages 8–12.

The New Way Things Work by David Macaulay (New York: Houghton Mifflin, 1998). A new edition of this classic visual guide to the wonders of machines. Ages 9–12.

The New York Public Library Kid's Guide to Research by Deborah Heiligman (New York: Scholastic, 1998). A complete guide to the skills students need to complete a research project—using the library, taking notes, conducting interview, evaluating sources, and more. Ages 9–12. Also check out the Web site: *http:www.nypl.org*

Index

A

Alien Encyclopedia project, 4, 100–108
American Heroes project, 74–81
Animal Adaptations activity, in Animal
    Inventor project, 33
Animal Inventor project, 27–35
Annual percentage rates, in Buying the
    Car of My Dreams project,
    55–56
A-OK checklists
    for beginning authors, 132
    editing checklist, 133
Art exercises, in Alien Encyclopedia
    project, 106
Assessment tools. *See also* How Did I Do?
    evaluation form
    as project component, 3–4
    purpose of, 1
Assignments, as project component, 3
Authentic learning, concept of, 1

B

Bar graphs
    in Buying the Car of My Dreams
    project, 62
    in School Census Bureau project,
    47–48
Buying the Car of My Dreams project,
    54–64

C

Card designs, in Did You Know? project,
    95–97
CD Information Plan Sheet
    sample sheet, 118
    in Software Design Company
    project, 114
CD-ROM, Software Design Company
    project, 109–126
Census data chart, in School Census
    Bureau project, 51
Census techniques, in School Census
    Bureau project, 46–53
Choosing Seeds and Soil handout
    distribution of, 11
    example of, 13

Classroom extensions
    additional learning through, 2
    in Alien Encyclopedia project, 104
    in American Heroes project, 76
    in Animal Inventor project, 29
    in Buying the Car of My Dreams
    project, 56
    in Did You Know? project, 94
    in Home Sweet Home project, 68
    in Kid's Seed-Starter Kit project, 11
    as project components, 4–5
    in School Census Bureau project, 48
    in School Sign Company project,
    39–40
    in Software Design Company
    project, 111
    in This Place Is a Zoo! project, 19
    in Trading Card Hall of Fame
    project, 84
Computers, Software Design Company
    project, 109–126
Computer screen form
    sample forms, 119–122
    in Software Design Company
    project, 115
Copyright concepts, Alien Encyclopedia
    project, 101–108
Cost analyses, in Buying the Car of My
    Dreams project, 60

D

Did You Know? project, 92–99
    exercise, in American Heroes
    project, 78
Distance Data Chart, in School Sign
    Company project, 42–43
Distance measurement, in School Sign
    Company project, 39, 41–43

E

Encyclopedias, Alien Encyclopedia
    project, 100–108
Experiential learning, as authentic
    learning, 1

F

Family portrait, in Home Sweet Home
    project, 68–69
Final product, importance of, 1

G

Germination, Kid's Seed-Starter Kit
    project, 9–10
Goals, project design and achievement
    of, 2–3
Group projects, value of, 4–5

H

Habitat, study of, in This Place Is a Zoo!
    project, 18–26
Hero, concept of, in American Heroes
    project, 75
Home Sweet Home project, 66–73
Hot Buttons
    sample form for, 123
    in Software Design Company
    project, 116
How Did I Do? evaluation form
    in Alien Encyclopedia project, 108
    in American Heroes project, 81
    in Animal Inventor project, 35
    in Buying the Car of My Dreams
    project, 64
    in Did You Know? project, 99
    in Home Sweet Home project, 73
    in Kid's Seed-Starter Kit, 16
    in School Census Bureau project, 53
    in School Sign Company project, 45
    in Software Design Company
    project, 126
    in This Place Is a Zoo! project, 26
    in Trading Card Hall of Fame
    project, 89

I

Individual projects, as whole-class
    activity, 4–5
In My Own Words exercise, in American
    Heroes project, 79
Interest calculations, in Buying the Car
    of My Dreams project, 55–62

K

Kid's Seed-Starter Kit project, 8–16

L

Linear measurement concepts, in School Sign Company project, 39

Living Things projects, 8–35
  Animal Inventor project, 27–35
  Kid's Seed-Starter Kit project, 8–16
  This Place Is a Zoo! project, 17–26

Loan payment chart, in Buying the Car of My Dreams project, 61

M

Maps
  My Special Place in Home Sweet Home project, 70
  in This Place Is a Zoo! project, 22

My Home is Sweet exercise, in Home Sweet Home project, 71

My Special Place exercise, in Home Sweet Home project, 70

N

Note-taking, guidelines for, 130

Numbers and measurement projects, 38–64
  Buying the Car of My Dreams project, 54–64
  School Census Bureau project, 46–53
  School Sign Company project, 38–45

O

Observations guideline, for Kid's Seed-Starter Kit project, 10–11

P

Package design guidelines, for Kid's Seed-Starter Kit project, 11

People and places projects, 66–89
  American Heroes project, 74–81
  Home Sweet Home project, 66–73
  Trading Card Hall of Fame project, 82–89

Pie charts, in School Census Bureau project, 47–48

Planting activity, Kid's Seed-Starter Kit project, 9–10

Plants, projects with, Kid's Seed-Starter Kit, 8–16

Posters, for This Place Is a Zoo! project, 23–24

Predator-prey interactions, in Animal Inventor project, 27–35

Predators, in Animal Inventor project, 31

Prey, in Animal Inventor project, 32

Principal calculations, in Buying the Car of My Dreams project, 55–62

Q

Quality standards
  in Alien Encyclopedia project, 107
  in American Heroes project, 80
  in Animal Inventor project, 34
  in Buying the Car of My Dreams project, 63
  in Did You Know? project, 98
  in Home Sweet Home project, 72
  in Kid's Seed-Starter Kit project, 15
  as project component, 1, 4
  in School Census Bureau project, 52
  in School Sign Company project, 44
  in Software Design Company project, 125
  in This Place Is a Zoo! project, 25
  in Trading Card Hall of Fame project, 87

R

Ranger Rick magazine, 4–5

Record What You Measure exercise, in School Sign Company project, 41

Research projects, 92–126
  Alien Encyclopedia project, 100–108
  Did You Know? project, 92–99
  Software Design Company project, 109–126

Resources
  bibliography, 134
  for Did You Know? project, creation of center for, 93
  location of, 129
  for projects, 128–134
  in Trading Card Hall of Fame project, 83

S

Scenarios for projects, purpose of, 1

School Census Bureau project, 46–53

School Sign Company project, 38–45

Seed-starting directions, for Kid's Seed-Starter Kit, 14

Self-directed learning, *vs.* structured learning, 2

Self evaluation. *See* How Did I Do? evaluation form

Signs
  in School Sign Company project, 38–45
  in This Place Is a Zoo! project, 21

Software Design Company project, 109–126

Soil analysis, for Kid's Seed-Starter Kit, 11

Standards of quality. *See* Quality standards

Structure, importance of, for elementary students, 1–2

Student handouts, purpose of, 1

Students, project goals for, 2

T

Teachers, project goals for, 3

Thematic unit, 4

This Place Is a Zoo! project, 17–26

Toffler, Alvin, 1

Topic selection
  in Alien Encyclopedia project, 103–108
  relevance as issue in, 1
  resources for, 128
  in Software Design Company project, 111–113
  in Trading Card Hall of Fame project, 83–88

Trading Card Hall of Fame project, 82–89

U

U. S. Postal Service, American Heroes project and, 75–76

W

Web Control form
  sample form, 124
  in Software Design Company project, 117

Web pages, in Software Design Company project, 109–126

What Do I See? Log, for Kid's Seed-Starter Kit project, 10–12

Whole-class activity, as project extension, 4

Writing assignments
  in Alien Encyclopedia project, 105
  A-OK checklist for beginning authors, 132
  A-OK editing checklist, 133
  In My Own Words exercise, in American Heroes project, 79
  planning guidelines for, 131

Z

Zoo Books series, 4–5

About the Authors

Phil Schlemmer, M.Ed., has been a teacher, writer, consultant, and curriculum designer since 1973. He currently works in the Holland Public School District in Holland, Michigan, helping to implement innovative instructional strategies. His work focuses on teaching students how to become self-directed, lifelong learners. He has previously published six books and many professional articles.

Dori Schlemmer has worked with local school districts to create specialized curriculum materials. With her husband, Phil, she writes books of teacher materials and develops workshop and conference presentations.

They live in Kentwood, Michigan, with their daughter, Erin.

Other Great Books from Free Spirit

Challenging Projects for Creative Minds
20 Self-Directed Enrichment Projects That Develop and Showcase Student Ability
for Grades 6 & Up
by Phil Schlemmer, M.Ed., and Dori Schlemmer
Give your students opportunities to explore beyond core curriculum by completing in-depth projects that promote lifelong learning skills. Reproducible forms help students choose and plan a project, report their progress and problems, keep record of their work time, and evaluate the project after completion. For teachers, grades 6 & up.
$34.95; 148 pp.; softcover; illus.; 8½" x 11"

Teaching Young Gifted Children in the Regular Classroom
Identifying, Nurturing, and Challenging Ages 4–9
by Joan Franklin Smutny, M.A., Sally Yahnke Walker, Ph.D., and Elizabeth A. Meckstroth, M.Ed., M.S.W.
Written for educators (and parents) who believe that all children deserve the best education we can give them, this guide encourages and enables you to identify gifted children as early as age 4 and create a learning environment that supports all students. For preschool through grade 4.
$29.95; 240 pp.; softcover; 8½" x 11"

Teaching Gifted Kids in the Regular Classroom
Strategies and Techniques Every Teacher Can Use to Meet the Academic Need of the Gifted and Talented
by Susan Winebrenner
The definitive guide to meeting the learning needs of gifted students in the mixed-abilities classroom—without losing control, causing resentment, or spending hours preparing extra material. Written by a teacher and field-tested, this book makes school more rewarding for everyone. Includes 30 reproducible handout masters.
For teachers, all grades.
$21.95; 168 pp.; softcover; 8½" x 11"

The Kid's Guide to Social Action
How to Solve the Social Problems You Choose—and Turn Creative Thinking into Positive Action
Revised, Expanded, Updated Edition
by Barbara A. Lewis
This exciting, empowering book includes everything kids need to make a difference in the world: step-by-step directions for writing letters, doing interviews, raising funds, getting media coverage, and more. For ages 10 & up.
$16.95; 224 pp.; softcover; B&W photos and illus.; 8½" x 11"

Jump Starters
Quick Classroom Activities That Develop Self-Esteem, Creativity, and Cooperation
by Linda Nason McElherne, M.A.
Make the most of every minute in your classroom by keeping this book close at hand. Features fifty-two themes within five topics: Knowing Myself, Getting to Know Others, Succeeding in School, Life Skills, and Just for Fun. For teachers, grades 3–6.
$21.95; 176 pp.; softcover; illus.; 8½" x 11"

To place an order or to request a free catalog of Self–Help for Kids® and Self–Help for Teens® materials, please write, call, email, or visit our Web site:

Free Spirit Publishing Inc.
400 First Avenue North • Suite 616 • Minneapolis, MN 55401-1724
toll-free 800.735.7323 • local 612.338.2068 • fax 612.337.5050
help4kids@freespirit.com • www.freespirit.com